T0368477

AuthorHouse™
1663 Liberty Drive
Bloomington, IN 47403
www.authorhouse.com
Phone: 1 (800) 839-8640

Published by AuthorHouse 04/08/2016

ISBN: 978-1-5246-0047-1 (sc)
978-1-5246-0048-8 (e)

Library of Congress Control Number: 2016904960

Print information available on the last page.

authorHOUSE®

Jack's Jobs

Jack's Hands

Jack's Hands

SPECIAL PEOPLE IN MY LIFE. WHO IS SPECIAL IN YOUR LIFE?

1. MY DAD MADE A LIVING FOR 10 WITH HIS HANDS.

2. MY MOTHER USED HER HANDS TO FEED, CLEANED, & DRESSED US ALL, WITH HER HANDS.

3. MY ONE BROTHER AND FIVE SISTERS WERE SPECIAL IN MY LIFE. ONE SISTER DIED AT 6 MOS. SHE ALSO WAS SPECIAL.

4. ALL MY TEACHERS WERE SPECIAL TO ME IN MY LIFE. TEACHING, ME KNOWLEDGE, TO, STUDY, MORE TO LEARN, ELECTRICAL, POWER PRODUCTIONS, ELECTRONICS, COMMUNICATION, MANAGEMENT, TO USE MY HEAD & HANDS WORKING, SENDING POWER TO MANY.

5. MY WIFE, SON AND DAUGHTER, SO VERY SPECIAL IN MY LIFE.

6. MY MILITARY BROTHERS & SISTERS, AND ALL CO WORKERS IN ALL MY JOBS HAVE BEEN SPECIAL IN MY LIFE.

7. OF COURSE ALL MY DAUGHTER IN LAWS, SON IN LAW, ALL GRAND CHILDREN, THEIR WIVES & HUSBANDS, MY GREAT GRAND CHILDREN ALL SPECIAL IN MY LIFE.

8. SPECIAL, FRIENDS, GERALD, BLACKBURN, WALKER, DAVID, HOOPER, GILL, & A HOST OF OTHERS WERE ALL SPECIAL IN MY LIFE.

9. MY MANY BUSINESS, CHURCH, CLUBS AND CO WORKERS THROUGH THE 80 YEARS 75 YEARS OF WORKING WITH MY MIND AND HANDS IN MANY JOBS WITH MY WIFE OF 60 YEARS HAS BROUGHT HAPPYNESS AND INTER JOY IN MY LIFE.

10. HOLD ON TO GOD, FAMILY, COUNTRY, FRIENDS, CO-WORKERS, ALWAYS LIVE FREE, FIND YOUR PLACE, KEEP GOING FORWARD. NEVER GIVE UP. WINNERS NEVER QUIT, QUITTERS NEVER WIN.

JACK JOBS PICTURES FROM THE WORLD ARE AN EFFORT TO TIE MY VARIOUS WORK LOCATION IN MY LIFE TO WORK JOBS OF OTHERS IN WORLD HISTORY. OR TO LOOK AT THE SITES OF THE NATURAL WONDERS ON THIS EARTH ALONG WITH WHAT MEN & WOMEN, BOYS & GIRLS HAVE JOINED THEIR HANDS TO BUILD. BIRDS HAVE THEIR NEST, FOX HAVE THEIR HOLES, PEOPLE THEIR HOMES, WITH IT ALL LIFE IS BUT A VAPOR LOVE, GROW, STUDY, COMMUNICATE, REST FIGHT, HAVE FAITH, FUN, TRUST, EAT, SLEEP, GIVE, TAKE WORK, TRAVEL, BY FOOT, BY CAR, BY SHIP, BY TRAIN, BY PLANE, BY HORSE, BY CAMEL, BY WAGON, BY RIVER, BY SEA, BY SKY, BY LAND, BY AIR, WE LIVE IN A TIME WHERE SPACE TRAVEL IS NOW HERE. FROM A FARM IN TENNESSEE TO THE LARGE CITIES IN THE WORLD. WORSHIP OF ONE TRUE GOD, OR OF VARIOUS GODS OR WORSHIP OF NO GOD IS WHAT LIFE IS ABOUT. TODAY IS MUCH LIKE OTHER TINE IN HISTORY. THE CHOICE BELONGS TO EACH IN LIFE. EACH LIFE HAS A CYCLE. MY LIFE CYCLE IS CLOSING DOWN, WHILE MY GREAT GRAND-CHILDREN IS STARTING UP, MAY THEIR JOBS BE JOYFUL AND THEIR GIFT BE FOR OTHERS AND MAY ALL SELECT THE ONE TRUE GOD. AND WHEN OUR DAYS AND JOBS ARE OVER MAY WE HEAR GOOD JOB, REST IN PEACE, WHO REALLY KNOWS WHAT THE AFTERLIFE HOLD FOR US? WILL WE BE ASSIGNED NEW JOBS WILL WE TRAVEL UP OR DOWN? WHERE DID WE START FROM, HOW WERE WE EDUCATED, AND WHAT DID WE DO RIGHT IN LIFE? WHAT DID WE DO WRONG IN LIFE? WHAT DID WE LEAVE BEHIND? WHAT IS BAD? WHAT IS GOOD? ARE WE ALL BROTHERS? BACK IN TIME WAS WE MADE FROM CLAY OR WAS WE FROM THE APE FAMILY? THE QUESTIONS ARE MANY AND THE PROCESS OF WHO WE ARE AND WHAT WE REALLY BELIEVE IS MOLDED IN BY WHERE WE HAVE BEEN AND WHAT OUR LIFE'S EDUCATION HAS FORMED IN EACH OF OUR LIFE. EACH WILL LEAVE THE EARTH AT LEAST JACK'S JOBS ON EARTH WILL BE OVER. MY AFTER LIVES AFTER JOBS WILL START?

MY HANDS HAS MANY SKILLS TO ACCOMPLISH MANY JOBS, THROUGH THE YEARS. IT ALL STARTED ON THE FARM.IN THE EARLY YEARS THERE WAS NO ELECTRICITY SO WE HAD HAND SAWS, HAND DRILL, HAND AXEHAND PICKS, HAND HOES, HAND SHOVELS, HANDS DID MANY TYPES OF WORK YOU USED YOUR HANDS AND FIX ALMOST EVERY THING WAS FIX WITH BAILING WIRE ON THE FARM. MY HAND DROVE A PAIR OF MULES AND AT 9 YEARS MY HAND WERE DRIVING FARM TRACTOR AND AT 12 YEARS OLD MY HANDS WERE DRIVING CARS & TRUCKS. PICKING COTTON, CORN, PITCHING HAY CUTTING WOOD WITH MY DAD WITH A TWO MAN CROSS CUT SAW. HANDS WERE USED TO HOLD PLOW HANDLES DIG POST HOLES AND 100 OF OTHER THINGS. HANDS SKILLS PERMITS THE ACCOMPLISHING MANY JOBS. MY WIFE AS A YOUNG FARM GIRL RODE THE CULTIVATOR WHILE DRIVING THE PAIR OF MULES PULLING IT AS HER DAD WOULD WALK BEHIND AND GUIDE THE PLOWS WITH HIS HANDS. MY HANDS. I GREW UP DOING FARM WORK, THEN WORKED IN STORES SERVING CUSTOMERS. THEN MY HANDS WERE USED TO PROVIDE ELECTRICAL POWER TO PEOPLE AROUND THE WORLD. THEN TRAINED TO PROVIDE SAFE LANDING AND TAKE OFF OF MANY THOUSAND OF AIRCRAFT AND THOUSANDS OF PEOPLE ON THE AIRCRAFT .THEN MY HANDS HELP, PROVIDE HOUSING TO THOUSANDS OF PEOPLE. THEN MY HANDS WERE USED TO PROVIDE SAFE MOVEMENT OF FUEL AND FOOD TO MILLIONS OF PEOPLE. THEN MY HANDS SENT ELECTRICAL POWER TO MILLIONS OF PEOPLE. THEN AGAIN MY HAND WERE AGAIN KEY TO SELLING HOMES TO HUNDRED OF FAMILIES.IN MY YEARS OF TOP SECRET WORK MY HANDS WERE USED TO PROVIDE SAFETY TO MILLION OF PEOPLE. THEY WERE USED TO TRY TO OBTAIN FUND FOR MILLIONS OF DOLLARS TO WORK ON NEW WAYS TO AGAIN DEVELOP NEW SYSTEMS OF NEW TYPE POWER SYSTEMS. AND AT 84 YEARS THEY ARE STILL WORKING .MY HAND HAVE BEEN USED IN MANY WAYS AND I THANK GOD FOR MY MIND AND HANDS .THEY WERE USED TO BRING CLEAN WATER TO THOUSANDS AND THE SYSTEM IS STILL WORKING IN MANY LOCATIONS OPERATING SO I LABOR ON STILL WORKING AND LOOKING FOR WAYS TO MAKE LIFE BETTER FOR THE WORLD. WHAT HAVE YOU DONE WITH YOUR EDUCATION AND HANDS? OF COURSE THERE WERE MANY CO WORKERS WORKING SIDE BY SIDE WITH ME IN MY EFFORTS AND MY WISH IS TO PAY RESPECT TO ALL PEOPLE WHO HAVE WORKED WITH ME IN MY 84 YEARS OF EFFORT. MY THANKS TO MY WIFE, MY CHILDREN, THEIR WIVES AND HUSBANDS,ALL OF MY FAMILY,MY GRAND CHILDREN, AND MY GREAT GRAND CHILDREN WHO'S HAND ARE WORKING TO HELP PEOPLE AT HOME AND AROUND THE WORLD . MAY GOD BE WITH YOU ALL. HAVE FAITH YOUR HANDS WILL SERVICE YOU WELL FOR A LIFETIME?

SNAP SHOTS OF MY LIFE JOBS RESULTS TO HELP OTHERS IN LIFE. NUTSHELL VIEWS FROM MY DAYS OF LABOR, ALL VIEWS AND NUMBERS ARE FROM GENERAL GUEST WITH PRAISE FOR ALL TEAM MEMBER AND CO-WORKERS, FAMILY MEMBERS, MILITARY BROTHERS AND SISTERS. MY HANDS WORKING HAD THE POWER OF TEACHERS, TRAINERS, ON THE JOB SKILL OBTAINED VIA PEOPLE AROUND ME HELP ME BECOME WHO I AM. IN NO WAY COULD I HAVE ACCOMPLISHED THE TASK WITHOUT MANY MASTERS GUIDING ME TO THE HIGHER SKILL TASK THAT PERMITTED ME TO GET UR DONE. EARLY YEARS. HOW TO MILK A COW. SET ON A STOOL BEND YOUR THUMB DOWN,PLACE YOUR 4 FINGERS AROUND A COWS TIT AND PRESS THE MILK INTO A PAIL, SPEED IT UP WITH TWO HANDS JUST ONE JOB BEFORE THE DAYS OF MILKING MACHINES. WITH MANY COWS AND MACHINES. THE MILK WAS THEN PLACED IN A CHURN PUMP THE CHURN HANDLE UP AND DOWN UNTIL YOU MAKE YOU'RE BUTTER. ALSO YOU CAN LOWER THE JUG OF MILK DOWN IN THE WELL TO KEEP IT COOL BECAUSE YOU HAD NO ICE OR ELECTRIC REF TO KEEP IT COOL. BY HAND YOU CUT DOWN A TREE, WOULD CUT BY HAND SAWS BLOCKS OFF THE TRUNK OF TREE, SPLIT THE BLOCKS INTO STICKS, SO THEY WOULD GO INTO A WOOD COOK STOVE FOR HEAT TO COOK, YOU HAD NO GAS OR ELECTRIC STOVES. LIGHTING WAS BY COAL OIL LAMPS BECAUSE THERE WAS NO ELECTRIC LIGHTS. MOST FOOD WAS GROWN RIGHT ON THE FARM. FLOWER, MEAL, SUGAR, SALT WAS OBTAINED FROM THE STORE. EGGS CAME FROM THE CHICKEN NEST. THE DAYS ARE GONE FOR THE MOST PART. NO MORE SMOKE HOUSES WHERE YOUR MEAT WAS STORED. YOU WOULD HEAT WATER ON THE STOVE AND TAKE A BATH IN THE WASH TUB. WATER WAS HEAT OUTSIDE IN A LARGE POT AND A WASH BOARD WAS USED TO CLEAN YOUR LAUNDRY, AND THEY WERE HUNG ON A CLOSE LINE OUTSIDE TO DRY. A METAL IRON WAS HEATED TO IRON BECAUSE YOU HAD NO ELECTRICITY .MOST OF YOU FARM FOODS WAS COOK ON THE WOOD STOVE AND CANNED ON THE FARM, MANY ITEMS WERE JUST SAVED IN DRY FORM FOR USE, MAYBE THIS WILL SHOW HOW IT USE TO BE.

JACK, S JOB, S TIME LINE MAJOR WORK AREAS.

1931-1937 BIRTH FARM LIFE. START OF MY FARM JOB'S AND SCHOOL YEARS, FARM JOB'S,FEEDING, MILKING, CHOPPING & PICKING COTTON, PLOWING MULES, DRIVING TRACTORS AT 9 YRS, TRUCKS AND CARS AT 12 YRS OLD, PICKING CORN, CUTTING AND BAILING HAY,BREAKING, DISKING, PLOWING COTTON & CORN, PICKING STRAWBERRIES, CUTTING WOOD, DRAWING WATER, PICKING AND STACKING PEANUTS. KEEPING THE CHICKENS FEED, COLLECTING EGGS. HUNTING, FISHING, KEEPING WOOD IN THE HOUSE FOR COOKING & HEATING.IN ADDITION TO FARMING, MY FATHER BOUGHT A COUNTRY STORE AND I HELPED RUN THAT ALSO FROM 1946 UNTIL 1949 AS WELL ALSO FARMING.IN 1949 .AFTER COMPLETING HIGH SCHOOL I MOVED TO FLORIDA AND BECAME ASSISTANT MANAGER OF A WOOLWORTH'S STORE IN MIAMI BEACH FLA. I RETURNED HOME TO TENNESSEE IN 1950 AND JOINED THE US AIR FORCE. I FIRST COMPLETED BASIC TRAINING AT LACKLAND AIR FORCE AND WAS ASSIGNED TO THE ELECTRICAL POWER SCHOOL AT CHEYENNE WYOMING. MY STUDY WAS BASIC ELECTRICITY, POWER UNITS AND PRODUCTION GAS & DIESEL UNITS, POLE CLIMBING.BUS DUCTS, TRANSFORMERS, CIRCUITS & POWER DISTRIBUTION A VARIOUS VOLTAGES, AND TYPE SERIES, PARALLEL, DELTA, AND Y CONNECTION. AFTER COMPLETING THIS SCHOOL I WAS ASSIGNED TO A USAF BASE ELECTRIC SHOP IN MOBILE ALABAMA. MY 1ST JOB WAS WORKING ON THE ELECTRICIAN LINE CREW. 2ND JOB WAS REPAIRING ELECTRICAL DENTAL EQUIPMENT, AND WORKING IN THE ELECTRICAL MOTOR REPAIR SHOP PLUS DOING ELECTRICAL P.M. WORK ON ALL BASE MOTORS, IN 1952 I WAS ASSIGNED TO GOOD FELLOW AIR FORCE BASE AT SAN ANGELO TEXAS. I STOPPED IN TENNESSEE TO MARRY MY WIFE MARGARET RUTH TURNER AND THIS WAS 24 FEB 1952 AND WE MADE THE TRIP TO CORINTH WHERE THE KNOT WAS TIED, 63 YEARS AGO TODAY IS 7 OCT 2015. ALSO THIS WAS THE BEST JOB I HAVE HAD EVER. PRODUCING A SON & DAUGHTER, SIX GRAND CHILDREN, AND TWELVE GREAT GRAND CHILDREN.

AT MY JOB IN TEXAS I WAS WITH THE MAINTENANCE OF ALL AIR FIELD RUNWAY LIGHTING AS WELL AS THE ELECTRICAL REPAIR OF ANY BASE ELECTRICAL PROBLEMS AT NIGHT, WEEKENDS, AND HOLIDAYS. WE REPAIRED ALL LIGHTING, POWER UNITS, AND I WORKED ALONE IN THIS JOB. ALMOSTGOT KILLED BY An IMPROPER INSTALLED POWER UNIT BUT WAS SAVED BY MY USING SAFETY HIGH VOLTAGE GLOVES, I DID HAVE WHAT LOOKED LIKE A BOLT OF LIGHTING FROM THE GROUND TO 2 FEET ABOVE MY HEAD. THIS WAS A FINE LEARNING ON THE JOB, TRAINING. ALSO GOOD TRAINING BEING MARRIED. OUR NEXT ASSIGNMENT WAS AT ROCKVILLE, INDIANA AT A NEW RADAR SITE. HERE MY JOB WAS A POWER PLANT OPERATOR WHERE I WORK SHIFT WORK ALONE OPERATING THE POWER PLANT. FROM THIS JOB I WAS ASSIGNED OVERSEAS FOR A ONE YEAR JOB AT SONDERSTROM AIR FORCE BASE GREENLAND .HERE I WAS PROMOTED TO SSGT.& PLACED IN CHARGE OF 22 ELECTRICIANS OPERATING THE BASE POWER PLANT, ALL BASE ELECTRICAL SYSTEMS, ALL RUNWAY LIGHTING, ALL SPECIAL LIGHTING, ALL GENERATING UNITS, LIKE TOWER LIGHTING, TRANSFORMERS, AND INTERIOR LIGHTING HEATING AND CONTROL SYSTEM. IT WAS NECESSARY TO ORDER A NEW LARGE POWER UNIT UNLOAD IT USE HEAVY EQUIPMENT,PULL IN INTO PLACE TIE IT TO THE ELECTRICAL BUS HOT AND AFTER I INSTALLED IT WE RAN IT FOR 6MONTHSWITH OUT SHOUTING IT DOWN TO MAINTAIN BASE POWER. WE ALSO FOUND WAYS TO REWIND ELECTRICAL MOTORS AND KEEPING THINGS GOING. I ALSO CLIMB 1200 FT. RADIO TOWERS TO REPLACE WARNING LIGHTING FOR AIRCRAFT. MY PRIOR SCHOOLS AND ELECTRICAL ASSIGNMENTS HELP ME ACCOMPLISH MY TASK HERE. AFTER I WAS HERE 6MONTHS I WAS PERMITTED TO FLY HOME WHEN OUR SON WAS BORN. THIS YEAR WENT BY SLOW FOR ME HOWEVER IT WAS A WONDERFUL TRAINING GROUND AND THE COLD AT 60 BELOW ZERO MADE OTHER LOCATION IN THE WORLD GREAT. WHAT A JOB. MY NEXT ASSIGNMENT WAS AT FORT GEORGE RIGHT AT SPOKAN WASHINGTON. HERE I WORKED AT THE ELECTRIC SHOP, AND AMONG OTHER THINGS INSTALLED A NEW TRANSFORMER BANK FOR UPGRADING POWER. FROM THIS LOCATION I LEFT THE USAF AND MOVED BACK TO TENNESSEE.WHERE MY NEW JOB WAS WITH THE GIBSON CO ELECTRICALCOMPANY. WHERE MY JOB WAS INSTALLING NEW HIGH VOLTAGE POWER IN WEST TENNESSEE IN AREAS THAT HAD NO ELECTRICAL POWER. THESE DAYS WAS BEFORE LIFT TRUCKS, AND POWER DIGGING TRUCKS .SO MUCH OF THE WORK WAS PURE HAND HOLE DIGGING, USING PIKE POLES TO SET ELECTRICAL POLES. LINEMEN USED CLIMBERS TO CLIMB AND COME ALONG WERE USED TO STRING POWER LINES. BOY HAS THIS REALLY CHANGED THE JOB. ALONG WITH GREAT TECH EQUIPMENT ADVANCEMENT COMES ALONG A REDUCTION IN JOBS. WITH BETTER FARMING EQUIPMENT HAS AGAIN REDUCED THE NUMBERS IN FARM JOBS. IN JAPAN I

WITNESS HAND REPAIR OF ROADS. WE USE EQUIPMENT AND REDUCE THE NUMBER OF JOBS.
AGAIN IN FACTORIES WHERE MANY PEOPLE ONCE WORKED THE JOBS BY USING EQUIPMENT
TODAY THE JOBS HAVE BEEN CUT SAY 1000 JOBS HAVE BEEN
REDUCE TO SAY 100 JOBS OK I AM JUST THINKING IN MY LIFETIME WHERE THE JOBS HAVE
GONE. WELL I HAD 90 DAYS FROM THE TIME I LEFT THE USAF TO REENLIST AND KEEP MY
RANK SO ON THE 89 DAY I STARTED TO WORK AT THE GIBSON CO RURAL ELECTRIC CO-OP.
THE FORMAN SAID JACK WHAT ARE YOU GOING TO DO? I SAID MARK ME GONE. I THREW
MY LUNCH BUCKET IN MY CAR, WENT HOME AND TOLD MY WIFE I WAS GOING BACK IN
THE USAF AIR FORCE, WENT TO MEMPHIS REENLISTED AND WAS ASSIGNED TO NASHVILLE
TENNESSEE STEWART AIR FORCE BASE, AND I WAS ASSIGNED TO THE ELECTRIC SHOP AND
MY JOB WAS WORKING ON ALL ELECTRIC SYSTEM FROM HIGH VOLTAGE, DISTRIBUTION,
AIR FIELD LIGHTING, INSIDE ELECTRICAL LOWER 110/220 VOLT AND MOTOR AND CONTROL
SYSTEMS, WIRING RUNNING CONDUIT AND ALL THINGS ELECTRICAL. MY NEXT ASSIGNMENT
JOB WAS TO THE ELECTRICAL SHOP AT ITAMI AIR FORCE BASE OSAKA JAPAN .MY FAITH IS
YOUR HANDS CAN FIND WORK AS MY HAND HAVE,TRAIN YOURSELF FOR WORK AND DO IT.

MY HANDS AT WORK STORIES. TIME 69 & 70 IN VIET-NAM

ON LANDING IN VIET NAM FOR DUTY IT WAS AT NIGHT AND ON THE WAY TO MY HUT LOOKING OVER TO MY LEFT OF THE BASE THERE WAS A PLANE WE CALLED PUFF THE MAGIC DRAGON MAKING CIRCLES AND TRACERS FIRE WHICH I KNEW WAS PLACING A SHOT IN EVER SQ IN OF THE GROUND AND THAT ALSO TOLD ME THE VIET CONG TROOPS WERE MAKING AN EFFORT TO COME ON THE BASE. ONE OF MY PRIOR WORK WAS BEING A ELECTRICAL ESTIMATOR AT EGLIN AF BASE (THE LARGEST BASE IN THE USA) WHERE I HAD WITNESS LIVE FIRE TRAINING WITH THE SAME TYPE PLANE. AT EGLIN IT WAS TRAINING ON DUMMIES. NOW THE FIRE WAS TRYING TO KILL REAL PEOPLE. IT WAS A KILL OR BE KILLED AND I WAS NOW WHAT IS KNOWN AS BEING A USAF VET IN A WAR ZONE. THIS IS KNOWN AS THE REAL DEAL. CLOSE BY. HOWEVER AFTER FLYING FROM TOPEKA KANSAS TO VIET-NAM I WAS SO TIRED I HIT MY BUNK AND SLEPT LIKE A BABY.

NEST DAY I FLEW TO MY BASE OF OPERATION AT TUE WA AND PUT MY HAND TO WORK AT THE JOB I WAS SENT OVER FOR AS NCOIC OF ALL OUR GROUND CREWS WORK IN SEVERAL GROUND LOCATIONS IN THE PROJECT OF MAPING NORTH AND SOUTH VIET NAM. WE HAD 3 MEN CREWS ON SITES WHO OPERATED 2 POWER UNITS, 2 RADIOS, 2 HIRAN SETS IN SUPPORT OF THE C-130 USAF CRAFT DOING THE FLYING AND MAP MAKING, AT THIS TIME WHILE FLYING THEY WOULD MAKE A 60 SQ MILE PHOTO AND WHEN THE PHOTO WAS MADE A SIGNAL WOULD GO FROM THE GROUND STATION MY 3 MAN CREWS WERE AT TO THE FLYING C-130 AIRCRAFT AND MARK THE MAP WITH IN 1/15 OF A IN OF CORRECT LOCATION. FOR THE 60 SQ MILE MAP. LATER WHILE MAPING IN SOUTH AMERICA WE USED FASTER USAF 707 AIRCRAFT, AND FOR SIGNLA USED A NEW SYSTEM CALLED SHARIN, NOW ALL THIS HAS BEEN REPLACED BY THE USE OF ORBIT UNITS MAKING MAPS FROM THEIR SKY LOCATION (GOOGLE MAPS)

WE USED MOSTLY HELICOPTERS TO MOVE THE MEN AND SUPPORTING EQUIPMENT TO THE LOCATIONS OF OUR 3 MAN CREWS LOCATION. MY LUCK HAS ALWAYS BEEN GOOD. ONE TIME I FLEW IN TO THE BASE ON A HELICOPTER FROM A SITE. AND STEPPED OFF. THE PILOT, A CHAPLIN, A MEDIC, A CIVILIAN, AND ONE OF MY AIRMAN GOT ON TO FLY BACK TO THE SITE, ON THE TRIP BACK THE TAIL ROTOR CAME OFF CAUSING A CRASH KILLING ALL ON BOARD. IT WENT IN THE OCEAN (10 MILES DEEP) AND ONLY ONE BODY WAS RECOVERED. THIS ACCIDENT HAPPEN IN THE 60'S PRIOR TO MY TIME IN VIET.NAM DEATH IS ALWAYS CLOSE ALWAYS THANK GOD FOR HIS PROTECTION.

JACK, S JOB, S YEARS 1931 TO 2011

1931 BORN IN TENNESSEE ON A FARM

1932 YOUNGEST IN FAMILY OF 1 BROTHER, 6 SISTERS.

1933 FARM WAS A RURAL AREA 10 MILES TO TOWN.

1934 MAIN CROP COTTON, CORN, MANY COWS, ECT.

1935 I STARTED TO GOING TO THE FIELDS LEARING.

1936 DAILY CHORES AROUND THE FARM.

1937 DAILY WORK ON THE FARM,

1938 STARTED TO SCHOOL, WALKED 4MILES X 2 WAY.

1939 HOME HAD NO ELECTRICY, WELL WATER ONLY.

1940 AT 9 I STARTED DRIVING A FARM TRACTOR.

1941 WORKING LONG HRS FARMING + SCHOOL.

1942 TRAVLING 10 MILES TO SCHOOL + FARM WORK.

1943 FARMING WORK, & MAINTAIN PHONE LINES.

1944 WAR YEARS PLACED HEAVY WORK ON ALL.

1945 I WAS DRIVING CARS, FARM WORK + SCHOOL.

1946 MY DAD OWNED A STORE I WORKED IN+FARM.

1947 SCHOOL, STORE, FARM WORK JOB, S

1948 HIGH SCHOOL + A JOB AT A SERVICE STATION.

1949 GRADUATED HIGH SCHOOL + MOVED TO FL, JOB.

195O SEVERAL JOBS + JOINED THE USAF & TEXAS JOB.

1951 SCHOOL, TEXAS, WYO, TRANING, ELECTRICAL JOB

1952 JOBS IN ALABAMA, MARRIAGE, TEXAS ELECTRIAL.

1953 JOBS ELECTRICAL & POWER IND & GREENLAND.

1954 JOBS GREENLAND & SPOKAN WA, + EXIT USAF.

1955 CIVILIAN ELECTRICAL TN, + USAF TN ELECTRICAL.

1956 TN.ELECTRICAL, MOVED TO OSAKA JAPAN.

1957 JAPAN ELECTRICAL MANAGMENT OF HOUSING.

1958 CLOSING OUT OSAKA AIR BASE+ OTHER WORK.

1959 HOME TO EGLIN FLA.MOVED SCHOOL TACOMA

1960 ELECTRICAL WORK & POWER PRODUCTION CAL

1961 MOVE, TO GERMANY ELECTRICAL/SECURITY JOB

1962 ELECTRICAL/COMMUNICATION TEAM JOB, S

1963 PLANING/ BUILDING/INSTALLING/SECURITY/JOB

1964 TEAM CHIEF, MAINT/INSTALLATION TEAM JOB, S

1965 ELECTRICAL ESTIMATOR FLA, SCHOOL/MISS.

1966 COMMUNICATION GROUND RADIO/NAHA, AB.

1967 QC /ELECTRONIC/RADIO/RADAR/NAGIVATION.

1968 COMMUNICATION-ELECTRONICS ENGINEERING

1969 GEODETIC COMM&ELECT, FORBES/VIETNAM.

1970 MAPING VIETNAM/BRAZIL JOB, S.

1971 USAF RETIRED/EXECTIVE DRICTOR COMMERCE.

1972 INSURANCE SALES/ELECTRICAL/ELECTRONICJOB

1973 OWNER/MANAGER HOME/SALES JOB, S

1974 MAINTANCE/SUPERVISOR APARTMENTS JOB.

1975 MAINTANCE/SUPERVISOR 7560 APARTMENTS.

1976 MANAGER GIBSON CO WATER DISTRICT JOB.

1977 LAYING WATER LINES BUILDING CUSTOMERS.

1978 OWNER TENNESSEE WORLD INC. PRESIDENT.

1979 BUYING AND REBUILDING HOMES.

1980 DEVELOPING A SUBDIVISON/ REFANACING

1981 OBTAIN 3.6 MILLION FHA LOAN JOB.

1982 LEFT MANAGER JOB AT GIBSON CO.WATER.

1983 CIVIL ENGINEER TECH/USA CORPS ENG, JOB.

1984 DISPATCHER OF 1/8 ALL POWER IN THE USA.

1985 BUILDING MANAGER GSA MEMPHIS TN JOB

1986 REALESTATE BROKER SELLING, HOMES, LAND, +

1987 INDEPENDANT CONTRACTOR STATE OF TENN.

1988 LISTING 56M, OF PROPERTY FOR SALE ERA RE.

1989 NEW JOB, ELECTRICIAN USA CORP OF ENG.

1990 LOCKING BARGES, REPARING SYSTEMS, MAINT.

1991 INSTALLING COMPUTERS, MANY LOCATIONS.

1992 PUMPING RIVERS DRY FOR MATAINANCE.

1993 INSTALLING NEW ELECTRONIC SYSTEM.

1994 UPDATING & MAINTANCE OF LOCK, S & DAMS.

1995 RETIRED, O2/10/95, USA, Coro ENG, NEW JOB

1996 BROKER FOR CRYE-LEIKE, NASHVILLE, TENN.

1997 SELLING HOMES/LAND/COMERICIAL/ JOB, S.

1998 SET UP OF SELL NEW SUBDIVISION 230 HOMES.

1999 DEAL COMPLETED 7 YEAR BUILDOUT, STARTS.

2000 1ST PHASE COMPLETED, 6 PHASES TO GO.

2001 SELLING/HOMES/LISTING/DOING REAL ESTATE.

2002 OBTAIN KENTUCKY REAL ESTATE BROKER LIC.

2003 LISTED 800+ LAND $12,000,000 M FOR SALE.

2004 SOLD 27 APTS 1.2 M, 68T GROSS PAYDAY.

2005 BOUGHT WEST TENN.HOME, MOVED JOB, S

2006 COMPLETED 230 HOME SALE BUILD OUT.

2007 REALTOR IN WEST TENNESSEE JOB.

2008 BOUGHT REELFOOT LAKE INN LLC 50 UNITS.

2009 SOLD PARTNER SHIP IN REELFOOT LAKE LLC,

2010 OBTAIN 20M CONTRACT JV INVESTMENT.

2011 JACKSON REFERRAL COMPANY BROKER.

2012 JACKSON REFERRAL COMPANY BROKER.

2013 PHOENIX PRINCIPAL BROKER

2014 PRINCIPAL BROKER PHOENIX & SAFETSTAR INC.

2015 PRINCIPAL BROKER PHOENIX & SAFETSTAR INC.

Early Farm Years Picking cotton by hands

Today Way

HANDS WERE THE WAY TO DO IT.

When I grew up on the farm about 8 years to 16 years old in the fall I would pick cotton by hand in the fall. My best day I picked by hand 412 pounds. It was placed in a Wagon to be pulled by horse or mules to a cotton Gin and baled in about 500 lb. Bails. This was my hands at work in the 40 & 50s. This was yesterday.

Tennessee's Top Crops

TNagriculture.com

SOYBEANS	CORN	COTTON	TOBACCO	WHEAT
Soybean production ranks first among all crops in Tennessee, with 43.7 million bushels harvested in 2010. Most are grown in West Tennessee, with Dyer, Obion and Gibson as the top counties. Soybeans are also the state's top agricultural export.	In Tennessee, corn is mostly grown for grain, but also a small amount for silage (livestock feed). In 2010, the state's corn farmers harvested a combined 685,000 acres, with an average yield of 117 bushels per acre (for grain) and 45 tons per acre (for silage).	Tennessee ranks eighth nationally for cotton production, with 387,000 acres harvested in 2010. Top cotton counties are Haywood, Crockett, Gibson and Madison, all located in the western part of the state.	The state's tobacco producers yielded 45.7 million pounds of tobacco in 2010, including burley, dark fired-cured and dark aired-cured varieties. Tennessee ranks third for tobacco production, and top counties are Robertson, Macon, Montgomery and Sumner.	Some 180,000 ac of wheat were harvested in 20 with average yie of 53 bushels p acre. Seeded in t fall and harvest in the spring, wh wheat is grown across the stat but primarily i Robertson, Gibs Haywood, Weak and Henry count

WHILE GROWING UP ON A FARM OUR MAIN CROPS WERE COTTON AND CORN. THE CORN WAS USED TO FEED THE FARM'S HORSES, COWS, PIGS, CHICKENS, GRINDING INTO CORN MEAL & CANNING FOR OUR FAMILY. OUR FARM RAISED SOLGUM FOR SYRUP, PEANUTS, CABBAGE, BEANS, TURNIPS, SWEET POTATOES, IRISH POTATOES, WATERMELONS, CANTALOUPES, APPLES, PEARS, GRAPES, PEAS, BEANS, WE ONLY NEEDED TO BUY FLOUR AND SUGAR. WE HAD OUR MILK, EGGS, MEAT AND IT WAS SAVED IN A SMOKEHOUSE, or HENHOUSE OR BARN WAS OUR STORE. IF YOU WANT A LIFE OFF THE GRID BUY A TENNESSEE FARM AND LEARN HOW TO GROW AND RAISE YOUR FOOD ON YOUR LAND. DURING THE GREAT DEPRESSION WHILE MUCH OF THE USA WAS GOING TO BED WITHOUT FOOD MY FAMILY WAS LIVING THE GOOD LIFE ON OUR FARM. WOOD WAS USED TO COOK & KEEP WARM. OUR LIGHTS WERE LAMPS WITH OIL. LATER YEARS WE HADE AN ICE BOX IN PLACE OF ELECTRICITY. WE HAD A BATTERY RADIO. ALSO A HAND CRANK TELEPHONE. I WALKED TO SCHOOL, OR RODE A HORSE BY HIGH SCHOOL WE HAD A SCHOOL BUS TO RIDE.

AIRPORT LIGHTING & CONTROL JOBS

MY HANDS WORKED TO KEEP LIGHTNING ON MANY AIRFIELDS, MOBILE ALABAMA, GOODFELL AIR BASE, TEXAS, IN GREENLAND, AND OTHER LOCATIONS, AFTER MORE EDUCATION I MOVED INTO GROUND RADIO & WORK WITH MY HANDS AT IN THIS JOB AT NAHA, OKINAWA FOR 3 YEARS, THE COMMANDER GAVE ME THE JOB OF QUALITY CONTROL OVER ALL GROUND RADIO, RADAR, GLIDE SCOPE, LOCALIZER, THE CONTROL TOWER, AND ALL EQUIPMENT WITH LANDING OF AIRCRAFT. THIS THREE YEARS WAS A VERY DEMANDING JOB BECAUSE OF ONE TURN OF A SCREWDRIVER COULD HAVE THE POSSIBILITY OF LANDING AN AIRCRAFT IN THE WATER IN PLACE OF THE RUNWAY. MAKE SURE ALL WORKERS HANDS ARE CAREFUL AT THIS JOB IN 1966, 1967, 1968 I WAS PROMOTED TO USAF SMS BECOMING IN THE TOP 3% OF THE USAF ENLISTED FIELD. WITH PLANES LOAD OF 300 PEOPLE SAFETY & QUALITY IS KING. THE JOY OF LANDING IS COMFORT TO CREW & ALL ON BOARD.

FARM YEARS WAYS

GROWING UP ON A FARM WAS USING YOUR HANDS TO FEED THE ANIMALS AS WELL AS CUT WOOD FOR FIRE, GROW CROPS PULL WATER FROM A WELL, AND BUILD A FIRE TO KEEP WARM.

WORK LOCATIONS CORP OF ENGINEERS

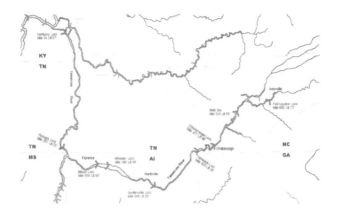

IN 1988 I WAS WORKING IN REAL ESTATE AND HAD 56 MILLION IN PROPERTIES FOR SALE.
I WANTED TO GO BACK TO A JOB WORKING WITH MY HANDS. I PULLED OFF MY SUIT &
TIE FOUND A JOB OPENING FOR AN ELECTRICAL WORK WITH THE US ARMY CORP OF
ENGINEERS, I APPLIED, PUT ON MY DIRTY WORK BOOTS & BLUE JEAN JACKET DROVE TO
NASHVILLE & WAS HIRED. MY MAIN JOB WAS AT CHEATHAM LOCK & DAM. I LATER MOVED
TO THE REPAIR PARTY AND WORKED AT MOST LOCATION ON THIS MAP. BECAUSE MY
ELECTRONIC BACKGROUND I INSTALLED COMPUTERS AT ALL THE FACILITIES ON THIS MAP.
MY LAST JOB WAS INSTALLING AN ELECTRICAL FIRE SYSTEM AT PICKWICK LOCK. MY THANKS
TO ALL THE ENGINEERS, AND WONDERFUL WORKERS KEEPING SUPPLIES MOVING ON THE
RIVERS.

DOWN AND DIRTY MY HANDS WORK.

IN MY YEARS WITH THE USA CORP OF ENGINEERS MY HANDS WORK WAS AN ELECTRICIAN INSTALLING POWER GENERATORS TO PUMP THE TENNESSEE AND OTHER RIVERS DRY TO INSPECT AND REPAIR LOCKS TO KEEP BARAGE AND ALL BOAT TRAFFIC MOVING ON THE RIVERS. I HAVING BOTH AN ELECTRICAL AND COMMUNICATION SUPENTANT LEVAL I WAS ABLE TO INSTALL COMPUTERS TO KEEP UP WITH ALL TRAFFIC MOVING THROUGH THE LOCKS. MY JOB,S WERE HARD MANUAL LABOR FROM MY AGE OF 55-65 YEARS AND THIS HARD DIRTY LABOR KEPT ME IN GREAT HEALTH AND PAID GOOD AND ALSO GAVE ME A 2ND RETIREMENT. IF YOU TRY YOU CAN ALWAYS,S FIND A JOB.

JACK, S JOBS 84 YEARS

0F W0RK By MY HANDS FARMING, MERCHANT, USAF, MANAGEMENT, IN CORP OF
ENGINEERS ELECTRICAL POWER/ELECTRONIC & WORK, WORLD WIDE, REAL ESTATE SALES &
DEVELOPMENT. PRESENT PRINCIPAL BROKER OF PHOENIX MANAGEMENT GROUP & .OWNER
SAFETSTAR INC.

THIS PHOTO WAS MADE ON THE SUNDAY AFTER OUR PRESIDENT JOHN F KENNEDY HAD BEEN KILLED THE DAY BEFORE. THIS PHOTO IS FROM CRETE. THERE WAS A SYSTEM OF PLUMBING HERE 4000 YEARS BC. MY JOB HERE WAS A REHAB JOB UPDATE ON ELECTRICAL, COMMUNICATION FACILITIES WORKING AS A TEAM CHIEF USING A TEAM OF HIGHLY SKILL PERSONAL. IT WAS A SAD DAY BECAUSE OF THE GREAT LOSS OF OUR PRESIDENT. HAVE FAITH YOUR JOB, S WILL LAST LIKE THIS PLACE.

WHILE DOING TOP SECRET WORK I WAS ABLE TO USE A PASSPORT AND FLY ON ANY TYPE
AIRCRAFT MOVING. DURING THIS TIME IN THE 60, S PAM-AM AND TWA HAD ROUND THE
WORLD FLIGHTS AND OUT OF THIS 3YRS ASSIGNMENT I WAS AWAY ON TDY FOR ABOUT
600 DAYS DOING ELECTRICAL, COMMUNICATION, and WORK. THIS WAS A NOT ONLY A
VERY HIGH TECH JOB IT WAS EXCELLENT WORK HOWEVER MY WONDERFUL WIFE CEO OF
THE HOME HAD THE TASK OF RAISING OUR TWO CHILDREN. SHE DID IT WITH A STRONG
HEART. HER JOB WAS TO MAKE IT WORK. SOME OF MY COWORKERS WIVES JUST GAVE
UP AND DIVORCED LEAVING THE KIDS FOR THEIR HUSBANDS. MY JOB WAS ALSO TO FLY
THE HUSBAND, S HOME. MY WIFE GETS THE CREDIT FOR HER JOB OF RAISING TWO GREAT
CHILDREN .HAVE FAITH THE PLANES WILL FLY.

THIS NEW CAPITAL OF BRAZIL AND IT WAS ONLY ABOUT 12 YEARS OLD AT THE TIME. THE STORY GOES, PRIOR TO THE PRESIDENT BEING ELECTED HE WAS MAKING A SPEECH, FROM THE BED OF A TRUCK, HERE WHILE RUNNING FOR PRESIDENT. HE ASK THE PEOPLE WHAT NEEDED TO BE DONE. THEY SAID BUILD A NEW CAPITAL HERE TO OPEN UP THE COUNTRY. HE SAID ELECT ME. THEY DID & HE BUILT IT. MY JOB HERE WAS TO REPORT BACK TO MY COMMANDER HOW TO CLOSE OUT OUR PHOTO MAPPING OPERATION IN THIS COUNTRY. AT THE TIME WE HAD VARIOUS POWER UNIT, COMMUNICATIONS, AND ELECTRONICS, USED IN AIRCRAFT MAPPING THE COUNTRY. THIS WAS A WONDERFUL USAF JOB. HAVE FAITH YOUR PLANS WILL TURN OUT FINE.

THIS WAS THE HOME PLACE AND THE OLD FORD. NO BATH, JUST AN OLD OUTHOUSE, A WELL FOR WATER, A BARN OUT BACK, BUT LOVE FOR ALL THE CHILDREN AND THE COUNTRY STORE ACROSS THE ROAD, FOR TREATS. MY SON AND DAUGHTER ENJOYED THE VISITS BECAUSE THEY HAD THE FULL TIME AND ATTENTION OF THEIR GRANDPA & GRANDMA. AS MY SON MOVES ABOUT THE SPLENDOR OF THIS WORLD SIGHTS I HOPE HE RECALLS THE GOOD EARLY DAYS WHERE PEOPLE HAD TIME TO VISIT. HAVE FAITH LOVE FROM EARLY TIMES WILL LAST FOREVER.

WE HAD MOVED FROM THE OSAKA JAPAN AREA AND ALSO MOVED OUR MAID WITH US TO OUR NEW BASE AT YOKOTA AIR BASE NEAR TOKYO. WE HAD A OPEN HOUSE . THIS WAS IN 1958, MY JOB HERE I WAS A ELECTRICIAN AND THIS WAS A LOCATION WHERE AS A S A USAF S/SGT I RECEIVED MY FIRST AIR FORCE COMMENDATION MEDAL,FOR MY JOB OF HELPING CLOSE THE AIR BASE IN OSAKA .

POWER JOB'S REQUIRE POWER RELAXATION MY SON HAS CHOSEN THIS WAY TO TRAVEL
AND THE HONDA GOLDWING IS ONE OF HIS TOYS .

1.ALL WORK AND NO PLAY MAKES FOR A DULL LIFE. FOR YEARS I WOULD TAKE A VACATION .
SOME WHERE IN LIFE I STOPPED MY VACATIONS. THIS YEAR AFTER 59 YEARS ON MARRIAGE
I PLAN TO START VACATIONS AGAIN. IT MAY ONLY BE TWO DAY A WEEK BUT AT 79 YEARS
I BELIEVE IT'S TIME TO START AGAIN TO RELAX. AFTER SEEING THE WORLD AND WORKING
MANY JOBS THERE MUST BE A WAY TO FIND RELAXING PLACES, PEOPLE, AND THINGS TO
BRING A HIGHER LEVEL THINGS TO DO. LETS SEE WHAT TOMORROW BRINGS? MAYBE I WILL
WRITE A BOOK ABOUT JOBS

MY SON MARK'S ONE JOB WAS IN CHINA HE IS IN THE RED SHIRT, WITH HIS CO-WORKERS. MARK WORKS FOR P&G. HE ALSO HELP BUILD A PLANT IN BELGIUM & WORKED THERE 4 YEARS. GOOD JOBS ARE FOUND ALL OVER THIS WORLD. I SPENT 12 YEARS AT JOBS OVERSEAS AND I, AM REALLY PROUD OF MY SON'S WORK NOT ONLY IN THE USA BUT OVERSEAS AS WELL. WHAT EVER YOUR HANDS FIND TO DO, DO IT WITH ALL OF YOUR MIGHT. HE CALLS IT A JOB.

THIS JOB TO BUILD THE LEANING TOWER , MAYBE THE WORK WORKERS WERE ON TWO MUCH WINE .THIS IS MAKING THE MOST OF A BAD JOB . WHY WOULD WE TRAVEL AND PAY TO LOOK AT A BAD JOB. MY WIFE IS HOLDING TWO FINE BOOK ENDS WE STILL HAVE. MY JOB AT THIS TIME WAS DOWN SOUTH IN ITALY WHERE WE WERE DOING A REHAB ON A USAF FACILITY INSTALLING NEW 3/PHASE ELECTRICAL POWER,INSTALLING NEW CABLE TRAYES,NEW WIRE MOLD,NEW CABLE TRAYS AND NEW COMMUNICATION WIRING NEW CONDUIT ALL IN A EFFORT TO KEEP OUR COUNTRY SAFE. THE PHOTO WAS OF A FAMILY VACATION TRIP. DEVELOPING JOB SKILLS PERMIT YOU TO WORK WORLD WIDE.TO OBTAIN JOBS ALWAYS DEVELOP AS MANY SKILLS AS YOU CAN.

THERE WAS A SAYING ALL ROADS LEAD TO ROME. HOW WOULD YOU LIKE THE JOB OF
FEEDING CHRISTIANS TO THE LIONS? IF THEY JUST HAD THE NFL THEY MIGHT HAVE
CREATED MORE JOBS, AND STILL HAVE THE CONTROL OF MOST OF THE WORLD. MY JOB
KEPT ME FLYING IN AND ON ONE TRIP THROUGH ROME I WAS ABLE TO SEE THE POPE & HIS
MOTOR GROUP IN THE AREA OF THIS PHOTO. ALL JOBS YOU MUST HAVE EDUCATION. TECH-
SCHOOLS ALONG WITH PRACTICAL SKILLS DEVELOPED ON THE JOB WILL TAKE YOU FAR.
GOOD THINGS COME TO THOSE WHO WAIT, IF YOU WORK LIKE HELL WHILE YOU WAIT. LOOK
AS IF EVERY DAY IS AN OPPORTUNITY TO DEVELOP YOUR SKILLS. HAVE FAITH YOUR WORK
WILL LAST.

My One Job required Me to relocate to Nashville Tennessee area for Work. I looked at many homes & placed a contract on this Historical home. It was built in 1926 & it was the Prior home of one of Springfield Mayors. Springfield has about 15,000 People & is the Roberson Co Seat. This was a short drive to Nashville about 600,000 people & is our state capital & known as Music City. This home boasts High ceiling's magnification decorations, beautiful Landscaping and a porch to visit neighbors on. Remember 3 things, location, location, location. 18 Years in a Wonderful Location. Easy walk to many places in town, Great living.

IN CALIFORNIA MY JOB WAS BEING THE ELECTRICAL SUPERVISOR OVER 12 ELECTRICAL MEN IN THE USAF AT NORTON AF BASE. WHERE THE TWO CARS SET, IN MY SPARE TIME HERE WE ALSO HELP BUILD AND WIRE THE CHILDREN DAY SCHOOL AT THIS SMALL CHURCH AND THIS WAS ANOTHER NO PAY JOB, I ALSO SERVED AS THIS CHURCH TRAINING UNION DIRECTOR. AT MY REAL JOB WE WERE OPERATING A SYSTEM WHERE IBM HAD A NEW HIGH TECH COMPUTER SYSTEM TO VIEW ANY INCOMING LONG RANGE DANGER TO THE USA. OUR POWER UNITS AT THE AF BASE RUN OFF NATURAL GAS 95% AND 5% FUEL FROM UNDERGROUND TANKS AND FOR SAFETY IN EMERGENCY SWITCH TO 100% FUEL FROM THE BURIED TANKS. JOBS ARE LOCATED IN MANY PLACES JUST WORK. FAITH AND WORK ARE TIED TO HANDS.

THE HOME IS THE 2ND HOME WE OWNED. ITS LOCATION WAS IN FORT WALTON BEACH FLA. MY JOB HERE I WAS THE ELECTRICAL ESTIMATOR AT EGLIN AIR FORCE BASE. THE HOME WAS BOUGHT WITH A VA LOAN. WE INSTALLED OUR OWN WELL TO WATER OUR GRASS AND SAVE ON OUR WATER BILL. ON OUR HOME HERE THE ROOFER WAS MAD AT THE PLUMBER, SO HE PUT A KEG OF ROOF NAILS IN OUR COMMODE .JUST TELLS YOU, WORKERS ON THE JOB'S OUGHT TO NOT TO BE MAD .MY THOUGHT NOW I SHOULD HAVE KEPT EVERY HOME I EVER BOUGHT. WE HAD ONLY A SHORT DRIVE TO THE BEACH FROM HERE. JOBS ARE AT HOME AS WELL AT WORK. HAVE FAITH YOUR HOMES WILL BE A RESTFUL PLACE.

FOR MANY YEARS MY WIFE HAS WORKED VERY HARD TO HAVE A FESTIVE TIME AT CHRISTMAS, THIS WILL BE THE SECOND YEAR THAT HER LITTLE ONE WILL NOT BE AROUND. LET'S HOPE BECAUSE CATS HAVE NINE LIVES SHE IS IN CAT'S HEAVEN. BECAUSE IT IS BETTER TO GIVE THAN TO RECEIVE. THERE WAS A TWO CONNECTION MARGARET WORKED HARD FOR THIS CAT. AND THE CAT REALLY KNEW IT. THE CAT WOULD NEVER HAVE MUCH TO DO WITH ME, OR ANYONE ELSE. I MISS THIS CAT. MARGARET DID An EXCELLENT JOB TAKING CARE OF LITTLE ONE. HAVE FAITH WE WILL LOVE ALL OF GOD'S CREATURES.

LET'S TALK RIVER JOBS. HAVING LOOK AT WATER WAYS AROUND THE WORLD, AND HAVING WORKED ON SEVERAL RIVERS IN THE USA THERE ARE MANY JOBS AVAILABLE ON BOATS, DAMS, POWER PLANTS, LOCKS, PUMPING STATIONS, COMMUNICATION, AND MAINTENANCE OF RIVER WALL, ON AND ON. MY WORK WAS NOT ONLY IN THE ELECTRICAL AREA I WAS ALSO TRAINED AS A LOCK OPERATOR ALONG WITH DRIVING WORK BOATS IN THE MAINTENANCE OF THE SYSTEM OF THE SYSTEMS USED TO KEEP ALL RIVER TRAFFIC MOVING. LOOK AT THE MANY PARTS NECESSARY TO KEEP EVERYTHING OPERATION. IF YOU LIKE WORKING OUTSIDE AS WELL AS INSIDE YOU MAY FIND WORK AT ONE OF THE MANY JOBS AVAILABLE ON SHIPS, ON THE SEA, AND THE MANY WATER WAYS AROUND THE WORLD. THERE ARE MANY FACILITIES THAT ARE OLD & NEEDING REPAIRS. HAVE FAITH YOUR HANDS WORK ON WORTHWHILE JOBS.

MY WIFE, MY CARE GIVER, OUR BACK YARD IN TN.

A proud Mother, My wife, our Son, & our Great-Grand-Daughter a Family as strong as the Big Oak Tree.

1. it's a real Job in our lives to keep and find time to come together on special days. The Job of preparing a special meal takes time planning and real work.2. As this 2010 year comes to a close for me I look back turning 84 years old, I have made a huge mistake wasting much money on a very bad business deal.3. I spent to try and obtain $ 20,000,000.00 thinking I was right and all along I was 100% wrong. I did get it from Dubai to a bank in Spain that folded, it's hard for an old dog like me to learn new tricks. Twice a child & once a man. Still working at 84 & its joy in every day. What next? My Faith is strong.

TO TRAVEL THE WORLD IS A JOB WORTH DOING, TO SEE YOUR CHILDREN GROW IS A JOB
SENT BY HEAVEN. THIS WAS A VACATION FROM GERMANY TO ITALY AND OUR TRUSTED 59
CHEV.

This was my temporary housing on one job in England Downstairs was a dining hall. This was at one time a girls school, The story is this man was standing by the grave of the priest who got one of the girls (fair Rosetta pregnant)they placed the girl in a wall sealed her 1/2 up and made the 400 girls walk by her until she died and then sealed her completely up. The priest was beheaded. Once a year you could see their ghost down by the creek. This was the Night. My crew had been drinking & one of my Crew, Threw out a lacing cord went down and tied it off by the creek. Then he placed a coat hanger over the cord. Then he placed a white sheet over the hanger. Next he placed an empty bottle in the sheet for weight, Then he went down to the dining hall where midnight dinning was in progress and talked up the ghost story. Then he ran back upstairs to wait for the men to exit. As they came out from midnight dining, he let the white sheet flout down the cord to the creek. The men coming out almost tore the door off getting back inside. My grand-kids like this story. Have Faith history teaches a good lesson

EVERY COUNTRY HAS SPECIAL PLACES MT.FUJI JAPAN. IS A SPECIAL LOCATION.1. MY USAF JOBS AND 3 YEARS IN THIS WONDERFUL LAND GAVE ME & MY FAMILY THE CHANCE TO SEE MANY PLACES. THIS PHOTO WAS MADE AS WE WERE MOVING FROM THE OSAKA AREA TO THE TOKYO AREA. I ALSO HAD THE CHANCE TO FLY OVER THIS MT. MY JOB WAS TO CLOSE OUT THE AIR FORCE BASE AND HOUSING AREAS IN THE OSAKA AREA. ON ONE TRIP I WAS THE ONLY PASSENGER ON A OLD 119 CARGO PLANE AND THE PILOT A NEW LT HAD A NEW CAMERA AND ONE WEEK EARLY HE HAD LANDED THIS PLANE SHORT OF THE RUNWAY AND TORE A HOLE IN THE TAIL. THIS WAS THE SAME PILOT & THE SAME PLANE IT LOOKED AS WE MADE CIRCLES AROUND MT FUJI IT MIGHT BE MY LAST FLIGHT. EVERY JOB HAS ITS DAYS OF REWARDS AND ITS DAYS FILLED WITH DANGER. LADY LUCK AND FAITH GAVE ME MANY MORE DAYS. Life is full of Joy and wonder.

Every great grandchild is special & like all snow flake. All not alike. .

1. Job in life is to train up a little one in the way they should go and when they are old they will not depart from it. My 28850 days on earth of working many jobs none are more important seeing your family expand and we hope our efforts will leave a better life for not only our family but all families. This is what life is about. Not just making jobs that take us through our days but paving the way for those who follow us. I HAVE FOUGHT MY BATTLES, I HAVE RUN THE RACE, MY LEGS ARE GETTING WEAKER BY THE DAY, I HAD A WONDERFUL PARTNER AND MANY FRIENDS EVEN WITH MAJOR BAD BUSINESS FAILURES I REALLY HAVE NO REGRETS, SAINT PETER WILL HAVE A LIST AND GOOD & BAD WILL BE WEIGHTED AT THE GATE. THEN I WILL KNOW MY JOBS REAL VALUE AND UNDERSTAND IT BETTER BY & BY.

1. I MARVEL AT THE JOB SKILLS NECESSARY TO BUILD A PLACE LIKE THIS.IN MY LIFE I WAS VERY LUCKY TO GROW UP ON A FARM. WE HAD TOOLS AVAILABLE TO NOT ONLY FARM WITH BUT. CUT TREES, DIG POST HOLES, BUILD FENCE WITH. CHANGE A TIRE ON A CAR, TRUCK, OR TRACTOR. ONE SUMMER MY DAD BUILT A BUILDING, ONE ROOM. AFTER CUTTING DOWN TREES SOME WERE HALLED BY WAGON TO THE SAW MILL. ONE BIG CYPRESS WAS CUT IN BLOCKS. FROM THE CYPRESS HE CUT OUT HIS OWN SHINGLES AND ROOFED THE BUILDING. MADE THE DOOR HINGES OUT OF LEATHER. MADE HIS DOOR LATCH HIMSELF HAD A LEATHER STRING YOU COULD LEAVE OUT IN THE DAY OR AT NIGHT PULL IT INSIDE FOR SAFETY ALL TOTAL HE HAD LESS THAN $50 DOLLARS FOR THE COST OF THIS WELL MADE ONE ROOM FARM HOUSE. IT DID NOT HAVE THIS DESIGN OR LOOKS HOWEVER LOOKING BACK I UNDERSTAND THE JOB MY DAD DID TO FARM, KEEP FOOD ON THE TABLE,AND DRESS A FAMILY OF 2 BOYS & 5 SISTERS +MOM & DAD HAD A CAR, TRACTOR, MULES, COWS, CHICKENS ON THE FARM. ON SUNDAY WE WENT TO CHURCH. WHAT A JOB. BY THE WAY SOLOMON'S TEMPLE'S ROOF WAS MADE WITH CYPRESS SINGLES THE BIG DIFFERENCE SOLOMON'S TEMPLE WAS FILLED WITH GOLD, MY DADS ONE ROOM HOUSE WAS FILLED WITH UNCLE FRANK, ONLY

MY JOB ALWAYS PERMITTED ME TIME TO VIEW AND STUDY THE FAITH AND BELIEF WHO AND WHAT PEOPLE WORSHIPPED. THIS PHOTO WAS FROM JAPAN WHO EVER HAD THE JOB TO MAKE THE ITEMS SURE HAD PLENTY OF SKILLS TO GO WITH BUDDHA.

ONLY WHEN YOUR JOBS TAKES YOU TO OTHER LANDS DO YOU UNDERSTAND HOW SKILL CRAFT MEN, HAVE BUILT OBJECTS TO USE AND BOND PRIDE FOR ALL TO SEE. I BELIEVE EFFORT IN EVER THING WE DO CAN HELP BOND ALL PEOPLE TOGETHER. WHAT WE SEE AND DO LEAVE A MARK. YOU GO TO JAPAN

MANY OF MY JOBS HAVE BEEN WORKINGS WITH HOMES. ONE JOB I WAS MAINTENANCE SUPERVISOR OVER SEVERAL HOUSINGS AREAS IN JAPAN. AT ONE JOB IN MEMPHIS I HAD 12 FOREMAN WORKING FOR ME AND DID MAINTENANCE ON 7246 APARTMENTS, SO THIS TEA HOUSE WAS OF IMPORTANT TO ME. THIS STORY IS THAT THE RULER OF JAPAN WOULD, IN THE SUMMER HAVE HIS MEN COVER THE HILLS WITH WHITE SILK SO IT WOULD REFLECT IN THE POOL AND LOOK LIKE SNOW, SO HE WOULD SIP HIS TEA, AND HAVE COOL THOUGHTS. WHAT A TEA HOUSE. HAVE FAITH YOUR TEA IN LIFE WILL BE GOLDEN.

4 GENERATION OF THE OF WORKERS 1. JACK 2, MARK
3, CASEY & TRAVIS 4. BLAKE. (TAKEN IN MARKS HOME).

1.WHEN YOUR JOB ASSIGNED IS TO GET READY TO DIE YOU START LOOKING FOR TIME TO MEET WITH FAMILY. MY MAIN JOBS HAVE BEEN MANY. MY NEW COMPANY SAFETSTAR INC I HOPE TO USE TO DEVELOP A SPECIAL ELECTRICAL SYSTEM THAT WILL BE A PORTABLE POWER SUPPLY THAT WILL COMBINE OR BREAK DOWN FOR MULTIPLE USE OR COMBINE LIKE A TRANSFORMER TO POWER HOMES & FARMS. 2. MY SPECIAL SYSTEM WOULD BE ABLE TO ALL LINK TOGETHER LIKE THIS. THE MAIN SYSTEM WOULD BE KEPT AT HOME, FARM, OFFICE, FACTORY, OR BUSINESS. THE UNITS WOULD FIT TOGETHER FOR MORE POWER OR BREAK APART TO POWER YOUR HOME, YOUR CAR, YOUR TRUCK, YOUR OFFICE, YOUR FARM TRACTOR, YOUR OFFICE, OR BUSINESS. WHILE SOME UNITS ARE BEING USED TODAY I KNOW OF NO PLAN TO MAKE MULTI ELECTRICAL PRODUCING POWER THAT WOULD UPLOAD TO VARIOUS LOCATIONS OR COMBINE TOGETHER FOR CENTRAL POWER INPUT WHEN NOT IN SEPARATE USE. THIS IS A NEW POWER UNIT DIRECTION.SAY TUINED.AT 84 YEARS I, AM STILL WORKING ON IT.

JAPAN GAVE ME ONE JOB TO TEACH ENGLISH TO JAPANESE BUSINESS MEN AT NIGHT. THIS WAS A NONE PAYING JOB, HOWEVER IT PLACED ME IN CONTACT WITH OF LEADERS AND IN TURN HELPED ME TO KNOW ABOUT THEIR COUNTRY AND IN MY DAYS OFF I KNEW WHERE TO GO. ONE OF THE LARGE BUILDINGS THE JAPANESE WOMEN GAVE THEIR HAIR TO MAKE A STRONG ROPE TO LIFT THE HEAVY BEAMS IN PLACE ON SOME OF THEIR BUILDINGS. AT WORK ONE OF MY WORKERS AT AGE 14 WAS BEING TRAINED TO FLY A PLANE WITH ONE LARGE BOMB ON IT AND IT WOULD BE A ONE WAY TRIP. HE WAS GRATEFUL THE WAR WAS OVER BEFORE HIS ASSIGNED TRIP.

BEST JOB IS TO HOLD A GREAT GRANDSON AND REST. 1. GROWING OLD IS ONE JOB THAT HAS ITS REWARDS. IT'S A VERY DIFFERENT DAY BUT THE PROCESS OF LOVE IS EVERLASTING. MY FAMILY LOVED ME. MY WIFE OF 59 YEARS & I LOVED OUR SON & DAUGHTER. THEN AS OUR CHILDREN HAD CHILDREN WE IN TURN LOVED OUR GRAND CHILDREN. THEN AS THEY HAD CHILDREN WE NOW HAVE A JOB OF LOVING OUR GREAT GRAND CHILDREN. WHAT I TELL YOU IS LOVE IS FOREVER AND THIS JOB IS NEVER CHANGING. OUR BODIES CHANGE, AND OUR SKILLS CHANGE TO THE POINT WHERE WE ARE INACTIVE MORE THAN ACTIVE HOWEVER OUR LOVE CAN STAY HIGH OR EVEN REACH A HIGH LEVEL. THIS LITTLE MAN BLAKE HAS MORE TOYS THAN A BIG TOYS STORE. HE HAS A LARGE FAMILY WHO ONE JOB IS TO PROVIDE HIM NOT ONLY LOVE BUT TOYS ENOUGH FOR MANY FAMILIES. WE LIVE IN A TIME AND THE USA CAN OBTAIN TOYS FROM ALL OVER THE WORLD. IF YOU LOOK AT LIFE TODAY IF WE BUY BLAKE A TOY IT MAY HELP SOMEONE IN CHINA BUY CAR FROM THE USA. IT CALLED WORLD TRADE. JOBS EVERYWHERE WHAT A WORLD. WOW.

MANY IN TODAY'S WORLD HAVE FORGOTTEN THE 3 AIR CORDER'S IN BERLIN GERMANY
ABOVE FROM THE 60, S .1. MY JOB REQUIRED ME TO FLY IN & OUT OF THIS CITY. MANY
TIMES AS WE WOULD FLY IN ON A CARGO OR PASSENGER USAIR FORCE PLANE, THE USSR
WOULD SEND FIGHTER PLANS AND BUZZ CLOSE BY. THE BERLIN WALL WAS IN PLACE WE
WERE INSTALLING ELECTRICAL & COMMUNICATION AND WHILE DOING THIS ON THE ROOF
OF THE BUILDING WE WERE ABLE TO LOOK OVER THE WALL AT GUARDS IN EAST GERMANY
ASSIGNED TO SHOOT EAST GERMANS TRYING TO ESCAPE TO FREEDOM IN BERLIN. WE
WOULD WAVE FREELY AT THE EAST GERMAN GUARDS. THEY WERE AFRAID TO WAVE BACK,
BUT WOULD HOLD A HAND DOWN BY THEIR BELT AND WAVE THEIR FAINIGERS ONLY. TO
BE FREE IS WHAT LIFE IS ABOUT. BEING ENSLAVED BY ANYONE IS TO BE DEAD WHILE STILL
BEING ALIVE .MANY PEOPLE IN THE USA DON, T UNDERSTAND HOW FREE WE REALLY ARE.
WE ARE BLESSED BY ALL THE BLOOD OUR MILITARY AND OTHERS GAVE JUST TO HAVE THE
OUR FREEDOM TO WAVE WITHOUT FEAR. GO USA!

MY SON ON A TRACTOR IN THE 50 & 60 THE SMALL FARMS IN TENNESSEE REPLACED MULES WITH TRACTORS. 1. MY EARLY JOBS ON THE FARMS WAS TO DRIVE TRACTORS LIKE THIS. WE COULD WORK INTO THE NIGHT AND ONE MAN COULD PRODUCE MORE IN ONE DAY WITH THIS MACHINE THAN WITH ONE WEEKS WORK WITH A TEAM OF MULES. COST OF THE EARLY TRACTORS FULLY EQUIPPED ONLY COST IN THE AREA OF $2000 DOLLARS. IT WAS A TIME OF CHANGE HOWEVER THIS DAY AND THIS JOB IS LONG GONE, SMALL FARMS HAVE BEEN REPLACED BY LARGE FARMERS AND LARGER EQUIPMENT. VERY FEW SMALL FARMS ARE LEFT .TODAY, S EQUIPMENT COST $250,000 PER UNIT AND UP. AND LAND NOW HAS GONE FROM 50 & 100 AC FARMS TO 1000, S AC AND UP TO 4000 ACRES. A VERY NEW BALL GAME. NOW GOVERNMENT HAND OUT TO FARMERS CHECKS ARE, TOP SECRET, SO IN PLACE OF A DOCTOR OR LAWLER, WE SEND A FARMER TO CONGRESS.NOW THAT IS PROGRESS, DON, T TALK ABOUT FARMERS WITH YOUR MOUTH FULL. HAVE FAITH FARMERS WILL FEED THE WORLD.

JACKS JOBS WHILE SELLING MOBILE HOMES TO DEALERS I WON A TRIP TO SPAIN & AFRICA .1.
ONE JOB I WAS A DISTRICT SALESMAN AND WON THIS TRIP FOR BEING A TOP SALESMAN,
MY WIFE & I ALONG WITH SEVERAL MOBILE HOME DEALERS WENT FOR TWO WEEKS TO SEE
WHERE THE QUEEN OF SPAIN SENT AND FUNDED THE SHIPS TO FIND AMERICA. SPAIN HAD
THE FUNDS AND YOU CAN SEE AND BELIEVE THE JOBS OF THE BUILDING THE SHIPS & THE
WORK ON SOME OF THE BUILDINGS STILL STANDING IN SPAIN. HAVING WORKED IN CIVIL
ENG, WITH BUILDINGS COVERING ALL AREAS LIKE, STRUCTURES,PLUMBING, ELECTRICAL,
HEATING, COOLING, WATER, SEWER, MATERIALS AND THE LONGEVITY OF HOMES & ALL
TYPES OF BUILDINGS. AT ONE TIME I HAD A JOB AS FORMAN OVER 7246 APARTMENTS
AND HAD 12 FORMAN WORKING FOR ME .WHEN I WAS SELLING MOBILE HOMES I WOULD
TELL PEOPLE BUYING THEM IF THEY DID NOT LIKE THE FLOOR PLAN, TO SLAM THE DOOR
IT WOULD CHANGE. ALSO TO PLACE FIRE CRACKERS IN THE ROOF, SO IF THE MOBILE HOME
CAUGHT FIRE THE FIRECRACKERS WOULD WAKE THEM UP SO THEY CAN GET OUT, A MOBILE
HOME CAN BURN IN 2 MINS. HAVE FAITH YOUR HOME WILL BE SAFE AND LAST.

MANY OF MY JOB, S HAVE BEEN IN ELECTRICAL LIGHTING .THINK OF LIGHTING ALL THESE CANDLES WHILE FLYING AROUND THE WORLD I LOOK DOWN AT THE LIGHTS, WHILE THINKING IF I JUST SCREW IN LIGHT BULBS I WILL ALWAYS HAVE A JOB. TYPES OF MY JOBS INSTALLING RUNWAY LIGHTS. INSTALLING HAZARD LIGHT ON 1200 FT HIGH TOWERS. INSTALLING ALL TYPES OF INSIDE LIGHTING .INSTALLING FLOOD LIGHTING. INSTALLING BEACON LIGHTS ON RIVERS AND AROUND AIRPORTS. INSTALLING STAGE LIGHTING. INSTALLING LIGHT TIMERS AND PHOTOCELLS FOR AUTOMATIC ON OFF. USING LIFT EQUIPMENT TO GET TO HIGH PLACES. USING HOST EQUIPMENT TO LOWER AND RAISE LIGHTS. IN GREENLAND WHITE FOX WOULD CHEW ON THE TAXI WAY LIGHTING PULLING THE LIGHTING FEED, S APART. SOME LIGHTS HAVE THEIR OWN TRANSFORMS, STARTERS ECT. THERE ARE MANY SIZE BULBS, TUBES, AND PARTS IN THE SYSTEM, SPOT LIGHTS, FLOOD LIGHTS, WATERPROOF LIGHTS, AND LIGHTS THAT KEEP TIME TO MUSIC. L LOVE THAT AIRPLANE PICKING UP SPEED TO ABOUT 150 MPH AND LEAVING THE LIGHTS BELOW. FLY ABOUT 500MPH SLOW DOWN AND LANDING AT ABOUT 150MPH SEE THE RUNWAY LIGHTS GREETING YOU BACK TO YOUR NEXT AIRFIELD.WOW KEEPING ALL LIGHTS BURNING CUTS CRIME. HAVE FAITH ALL LIGHTS WILL KEEP BURNING.

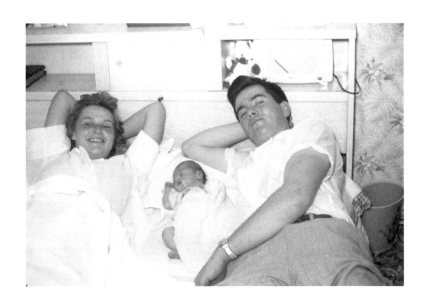

MOTHER MARGARET, SON MARK LEE AND NEW DAD JACK .THE USAF HAD ALLOWED ME
TO FLY HOME FROM GREENLAND FOR OUR SONS BIRTH. YOU WILL NEVER FIND A BETTER
JOB, THAN BEING AT THE BIRTH OF YOUR CHILD. AFTER A WEEK I WAS BACK IN GREENLAND
FOR SIX MORE MONTHS AT MY REAL JOB. FAMILY BONDS ARE REALLY WHAT HOLDS OUR
WORLD TOGETHER. WHEN I CAME HOME WE BOUGHT A 1950 FORD BUSINESS COUPE,
PLACED MARKS BABY BED IN THE BACK, AND LEFT TENNESSEE FOR MY NEW JOB IN SPOKAN
WASHINGTON.MARK WOULD SLEEP ALL DAY AND CRIED ALL NIGHT IN THE MOTEL. IT MADE
HIM STRONG. THIS SON IS NOW 60 AND HIS HAND ARE WORKING AS A PROJECT MANAGER
BUILDING PLANTS TO MFG FOOD TO FEED THE WORLD. HAVE FAITH ALL HANDS WILL WORK
FOR GOOD.

THE YEAR WAS 1952 -1953 PHOTO WAS THE ICE CAP.

1. The USAF sent me A. Through Basic training in Texas. B. Sent me for 6mo through, tech school (Electrical power production, pole climbing, in Wyo) C. Next I was sent to a USAF base in Alabama. While Here I RECEIVED MORE electrical experienced. My next assignment was working at a flight training base in TEXAS. My major job here was in the Maintained and operation of the Air field lighting and while working alone at night came very close to being killed because of an improper installed power generator that made a feedback to the airfield lighting that should have been dead. My next assignment was in Indian, Here I was a power plant operator (providing electrical power to a new Radar Site,) F, At this new job in Greenland I was promoted to Staff SSgt, Placed in charge of 20 USAF AIRMAN WHERE I RAN THE POWER PLANT, ALL AIRFIELD LIGHTING, ALL BASE ELECTRICAL DISTRIBUTION AND ALL POWER SYSTEM SUPPORTING OFF BASE FACILITATED. WHILE HERE I also was trained to kill a polar bear, you would cut a hole in the Ice, place peas around the hole, when the bear would come up to take a pea you would then kick him in the Ice hole.

MARRIAGE, HEATHER TO CASEY FREEMAN, HAS NOW PRODUCED OUR NEWEST GREAT
GRANDSON CONNER LEE FREEMAN 5 YEARS, OLD. CASEY JOB IS WITH LOWES, WHILE
HEATHER WORKS AT JACKSON STATE COLLEGE. THE SMALL STATE COLLEGE IS THE 1ST LINE
OF EDUCATION OF MOVING PEOPLE TO BETTER JOB'S. WHILE MANAGING THE GIBSON CO
WATER DISTRICT, I USED MY GI BILL, AND NIGHT CLASS TO STUDY ACCOUNTING, AND REAL
ESTATE LAW WHILE OBTAINING VITAL CREDITS TO MOVE UP TO A REAL ESTATE BROKER,
I WAS SIDE TRACKED WHILE WORKING FOR TEN YEARS UNTIL I BECAME 65 YEARS OLD
RETIRING FROM THE US ARMY CORP OF ENGINEERS,THEN MOVING INTO MY NEW JOB
AS A REAL ESTATE BROKER AND USING MY EDUCATION I HAD GAINED 1O YEARS PRIOR.
EDUCATION IS A BUILDING BLOCK THAT STAYS WITH YOU FOR LIFE. ALWAYS LOOK FOR WAY
TO MOVE UP AND ALL WAYS LOOK TO FIND WAYS TO MAKE LIFE BETTER FOR EVERY ONE IN
LIFE. I WAS INVOLVED IN HELPING SELL AND BUILD 236 HOMES AND RECEIVED PAY FOR MY
EFFORTS OVER A 7 YR PERIOD OF TIME. WOW WHAT A JOB.

JACKS FAMILY, JACKS JOBS, A VISIT HOME .BACK ROW1. JACK FREEMAN, FRANKLIN POWELL, GEORGE FREEMAN, BESSIE FREEMAN, JAMES LASTER MAMIE FREEMAN, EUGENE FREEMAN LOWER ROW CARROL POWEL, VIRGINIA FREEMAN, WILMA POWELL, MARGARET FREEMAN, RUTH LASTER, CONNIE LASTER, MARK FREEMAN GEORGE NEIL FREEMAN & BETTY LUE POWELL. ALL IN THE BACK ROW BUT MYSELF & JAMES ARE NOW GONE + WILMA & RUTH. THE JOB I WISH TO TELL YOU ABOUT. WHEN I FIRST GOT OUT OF HIGH SCHOOL, FRANK POWEL HAD WORKED AT THE LOCAL MILL FOR YEARS AND I RECEIVED HIS HELP TO OBTAIN ME A JOB IN THE MILL. THE MILL MADE HAM BAGS AND I HAD TO HELP KEEP THE MACHINES RUNNING. I WORKED AT THIS FOR 3 WEEKS AND THE CHANGING OF BROKEN PARTS IN THE MACHINES WAS PURE MADNESS TO ME. THE COTTON FLYING IN THE AIR, AND THE THOUGHT OF BEING HERE FOR LIFE WAS NO LIFE FOR ME. MY BROTHER IN LAW FRANKLIN AND MY SISTER WILMA SPENT THEIR LIFE AND BOTH RETIRED FROM HERE. IT LET THEM PUT THEIR TWO DAUGHTERS CAROL & BETTY THROUGH COLLEGE. BETTY HAS RECENTLY RETIRED FROM TEACHING 2ND GRADE .MY JOB WAS TO BREAK FROM THE MILL AND TRAVEL THE WORLD.

My Wife, Margaret, with two of our Grandson, Josh & Travis at another Grandson Casey's Weddings. PLENTY OF JOBS TO TALK ABOUT HERE. When we married Margaret was working in the office of the Brown Shoe Company in Trenton Tennessee. This was the shipping center for many smaller shoe factories in Tennessee. After our marriage she worked another month before moving to Texas where I was station. Now all the good Brown shoe factory Jobs have Left Tennessee, all factory's closed. Many factory's empty now. Hard to complete with .50 Cents per Hr. Labor from overseas. We now live in a throw away shoe time, hard to find a shoe repair shop in Tennessee. Changing World, Changing work jobs location. Many US Company's now building factory's overseas. Some overseas company building factory's here in Tennessee. Is all jobs changing location? Is the One World job market becoming a reality? My son building plants worldwide said his company stock lost him big dollars last week. This was his retirement funds .Will it come back? Maybe it depends on his and others in his company ability to perform as a Team worldwide to make a profit and for his stock to do well. In life whatever our job performance pays. Have faith any marriage will last a lifetime.

JACKS JOB AT THIS TIME WAS ELECTRICAL SCHOOL.1.I WAS IN SCHOOL, BEING TRAINED BY A CONTRACT IN ELECTRICAL POWER GENERATION & STABLE MOTOR GENERATORS SETS, ALONG WITH LARGE 400 HP AIR UNITS ALL TO SUPPORT A NEW IBM COMPUTER SYSTEM WHERE PERSONNEL WOULD USE TO CHECK ANY INCOMING ICBM SYSTEM TO PROTECT THE USA. THIS WAS THE 1ST HOME WE BOUGHT AND IT WAS LOCATED IN TACOMA WASHINGTON. IT COST WAS $13,000 & I SOLD MY CAR FOR THE DOWN PAYMENT AND BOUGH AN OLD JUNKER TO DRIVE TO SCHOOL. I ALSO OBTAINED SIDE ELECTRICAL JOBS FOR EXTRA INCOME, MY BIG JOB WAS TO COVER OUR YARD WITH SAWDUST PRIOR TO PLACING FILL DIRT TO ALLOW THE YARD TO GROW BEFORE THE DIRT WOULD FILTER INTO THE ROCKS. AFTER COMPLETING SCHOOL HERE, I WAS ASSIGNED TO A NEW LOCATION SITE AT NORTON AIR FORCE BASE. WE WERE ABLE TO SELL OUR 1ST HOME FOR ENOUGH PROFIT TO BUY A NEW 1959 CHEV AUTO. WE DROVE IT TO CALIFORNIA, HOME TO TENNESSEE, BACK TO CALIF, THEN TO NEW YORK, SHIPPED IT TO GERMANY FOR 3 YRS, SHIPPED IT BACK TO NEW YORK, AND DROVE IT FROM NEW YORK TO OUR NEW BASE EGLIN AFB FLA...JOBS, HOMES, CARS ALL PART OF WORKING .WOW WHAT A LIFE.

TOMMIE FREEMAN MY SON, S WIFE HAS A JOB HISTORY AS STRONG AS THE BIG REDWOOD TREES.

1 TOMMIE NOW WORKS FOR P & G HOWEVER ABOUT 3 YEARS AGO SHE WENT BACK TO SCHOOL AND OBTAIN HER MASTERS DEGREE TO BE READY FOR A BETTER JOB IN YEARS TO COME. MANY JOB, S ARE ALWAYS AVAILABLE WHILE MORE EDUCATION ALWAYS MAKES YOU STRONGER LIKE THE BIG REDWOOD AND OPENS UP MORE JOB, S. EVERY BIT OF EDUCATION I RECEIVED IN MY LIFE ALWAYS OPEN MORE JOB, S FOR ME. AS I ATTENDED MORE SCHOOLS AND EDUCATION I WAS ABEL TO BID ON MORE AND BETTER JOBS. AS I BECAME EDUCATED IN REAL ESTATE AGAIN I WAS ABLE TO MOVE UP AGAIN TO A BROKER STATUS IN BOTH TENNESSEE AND KENTUCKY. THIS OPEN UP THE POWER TO BETTER SALES. KNOWLEDGE IS POTENTIAL POWER. LIKE A BIG ELECTRICAL GENERATOR IT IS USELESS UNLESS IT IS RUNNING AND PRODUCING POWER. MANY PEOPLE LIKE HENRY FORD HAD LITTLE FORMAL EDUCATION, HE EDUCATED HIMSELF. MY SON HAS A GREAT JOB, AND HE LIKE FORD EDUCATED HIMSELF. WHAT A JOB.

LONDON WAS A PLACE ON THE WAY TO MY JOB.

WHILE BUILDING A NEW FACILITY IN ENGLAND I HAD THE CHANCE TO VISIT LONDON
SEVERAL TIMES. EVERY JOB WE WORK IN LIFE BRINGS THE OPTIONS TO SEE MANY THINGS.
ENGLAND AND JAPAN THE TRAFFIC MOVES ON THE LEFT SIDE OF THE ROAD. BEING TEAM
CHIEF OF A MASSIVE JOB ALSO PERMITS YOU TWO SIDES BOTH RIGHT & LEFT WAYS TO
OPERATE .I SEE THE WAY TO ACCOMPLISH YOUR BEST TEAM EFFORT IS TO BRING WORKERS
TOGETHER LIKE SINGING ON THE SAME PAGE . IN THIS JOB WE INSTALLED LARGE CABLE
TRAYS, LARGE 3 PHASE POWER SYSTEMS. MANY RF CABLES FROM NEW TYPE ANTENNAS,
MANY MILES OF COMMUNICATIONS WIRE. WIRE MOLD,CONDUIT BRING POWER FROM THE
BUS DUCT VIA CIRCUIT BREAKERS TO THE EQUIPMENT ON ONE SIDE, COMMUNICATION
WIRES ON THE OTHER SIDE WHERE MANY WORKERS WOULD WORK THEIR STATIONS 24 HRS
PER DAY,7 DAYS PER WEEK. TIME IS ALWAYS IMPORTANT SO SIGNALS FROM ATOMIC CLOCKS
WAS WIRED TO EACH STATION. TRAINED SKILLED HANDS FROM MANY TRADES WORKING
TOGETHER CAN BRING OUTSTANDING ACCOMPLISHMENTS IN RECORD TIME IF THE TEAM
IS ON THE SAME SIDE OF THE ROAD. VISIT WWW.CHICKSNDS.COM GO TO THE GALLEY OF
PHOTOS AND LOOK AT THE FLAR 9 SYSTEMS. WHAT A JOB

BOATS AT ONE TIME PRODUCED MANY JOBS IN THE MOVEMENT OF PEOPLE. THERE IS STILL SOME IN USE HOWEVER MANY ARE NOW GONE.NOW WE HAVE THE SUPER SHIPS LIKE A CITY CRUISING THE SEAS & THEY CREATE MANY JOB'S .SAME WITH PLANES IN MY EARL DAYS OF C47 & C54 50 TO 100 PASSENGERS WERE IT. NOW 250 & 300 PASSENGERS & MORE ARE DAILY THINGS. PASSENGERS TRAINS I TRAVEL ON ARE ALMOST A THING OF THE PAST. WHY? BECAUSE? LOOK AT ALL THE DEAD STATIONS IN TOWNS IN THE USA. I LOVED TO RIDE A BUS. FEW NOW RUNNING. NOW. AT ONE TIME IN OUR LIFE ONE CAR WAS IT. NOW IT'S A ONE CAR PER PERSON. WHY. ? IT BECAUSE. ONLY A FEW PLACES LEFT WITH HORSE DRAWN OR TRACTOR USED FOR FAMILY HIGHWAY TRANSPORTATION. YES I RODE A HORSE 4 MILES TO SCHOOL AND 4 MILES HOME THOSE DAYS ARE GONE. HAVE FAITH TRANSPORTATION IS AVAILABLE.

A NEW CITY FROM THE AIR LOOKS LIKE, S an AIR PLANE

A MAN I MET IN JAPAN TOLD ME ABOUT THIS NEW CITY. I HAD READ A BOOK THE MAGIC OF BELIEF BY HOW BELIEVING YOUR THOUGHTS WOULD MAKE IT HAPPEN. I BEGAN TO PUT IT TO PRACTICE. MAKING A LONG STORY SHORT TAKING A NUMBER OF STEPS AND IN ABOUT A YEARS TIME & AFTER A SIDE TRIP TO VIETNAM I WOUND UP HERE ON A SUNDAY MORNING AND WAS ABLE TO SPEAK IN A LARGE CHURCH . IT WAS A SPECIAL TIME FOR ME TO HAVE ARRIVED IN THIS NEW CAPITAL CITY IN BRAZIL .TO ME YOUR THOUGHTS CAN REALLY COME TRUE IF YOU WORK AT IT. THOUGHTS LINK TO ACTIONS BRINGS ABOUT WONDERS THAT MANY PEOPLE ONLY DREAM ABOUT, I ASK YOU TO BELIEVE AND ACT TO MAKE THINGS HAPPEN. IF I RECALL THE AUTHOR OF THE MAGIC OF BELIEF WAS BRISTAL MYERS. FAITH AND BELIEF ARE TIED TOGETHER LIKE, THOUGHT CHAINED TO ACTION. YOU TRY IT, JACK'S JOB'S ALWAYS IN THE MIX. THE PRESIDENT OF BRAZIL WAS MAKING A SPEECH FROM THE BACK OF A TRUCK AND ASK WHAT WILL HELP? THE PEOPLE   SAID MOVE THE CAPITAL HERE, THEY ELECTED HIM AND HE DID IT. WHAT A GOOD JOB. HEARING PEOPLE AND DOING THE RIGHT THING. HAVE FAITH YOUR DREAMS WILL COME TRUE.

01.31.2010 09:55

JOB,S FEEDING THE BIRDS EACH DAY THEY EXPECT IT.

1. FOR 73 YEARS OF MY 79 YEARS I HAVE WORKED I HAVE WORKED MANY HRS AT VARIOUS JOBS, MANY JOBS I WORKED 7 DAYS A WEEK AT LEAST 10 HRS PER DAY. SO THE EARLY JOBS, PAID VERY LITTLE, MANY DAYS WAS NO PAY FARM DAYS. SAY MY JOB PICKING STRAWBERRIES I RECEIVED .03 CENTS PER QUART. OR PICKING COTTON IT WAS PAY BY THE POUNDS PICKED. MY BEST DAY I PICKED 412 LBS. I REALLY DO NOT REMEMBER THE PRICE PAID BY POUND HOWEVER IT WAS ONLY A FEW DOLLARS. AS I MOVED INTO WORK AS A MASTER ELECTRICIAN WITH PAY AS AGREED TO BY THE BROTHERHOOD OF ELECTRICAL WORKERS PAY WAS MUCH BETTER. MANY JOBS ALSO HAD PERKS LIKE A PROVIDED TRUCK OR CAR AND ALL TRAVEL, FOOD, MOTEL, AND ALL FEES, TAX, PAID. SOME JOB,S LIKE BEING REAL ESTATE BROKER ITS A PURE COMMISSION PAY FOR EXAMPLE I SOLD 1.2 MILLION OF APARTMENT AND RECEIVED GROSS $68,000 MY PART WAS $48,000 FOR 3 HOURS WORK THATS WAS ABOUT $16,000 PER HOURS HOWEVER I HAD TO PAY MANY ITEMS OF EXPENSES FROM THIS. AND THESE TYPE SALES ARE FEW AND FAR APART. LIKE THE BIRDS WHO EXPECT THEIR FOOD IN HOT OR COLD MANY EXPECT THEIR TAKE FROM THE PROCESS. WORK FOR THE NIGHT IS COMING WHEN MAN WORKS NO MORE. MY TIME AND JOBS ARE RUNNING OUT. I NOW HAVE IBM NO CURE, NO TREATMENT, IT MEANS I WILL NOT BE ABLE TO WALK OR EAT. I MUST WORK QUICK NOW. I HAVE WORKED 14,600 HRS PER YEAR x 73 YEARS = 1,065,800 HRS AT $5 PER HR IS $5,239,000 ESTIMATE INCOME SHOT. SO WHAT?

PART OF THE COFFEE CLUB AT OUR HOME 06/25/2011 JACKSON TN.

STANDING RIGHT TO LEFT JACK, RAY, DR. TODD, PROF SCOTT, TOM, JC, PREACHER JOHN, BOB, SEATED RIGHT TO LEFT JAMES, GRADY, JOHN, AND JOE DAY. MEETING AT HIGHLAND McDONALD MONDAY THROUGH FRIDAY 8:00 TILL 9:00 PLUS TO PLAN THE DIRECTION OUR WORLD WILL GO OR REARRANGE WHERE IT HAS BEEN. MOST ARRIVE RIDING A GRIZZLY BEAR WHIPPING IT WITH A RATTLER SNAKE LOOKING FOR A CUP OF BLACK HOT BIG Mc SENIOR COFFEE. AND A OLD OR NEW JOKE. AND WHO DIED LAST NIGHT, AND WHERE THE STOCK MARKET IS AT. MISSING MEMBER WILL REPORT AT LATER MEETINGS. THE BEST THINK TANK IN JACKSON TN.

MY WIFE'S FAMILY, LEFT TO RIGHT, DORTHY, JAMES,MILDRED, MR ADAMS, MYRA, J.D, DEMETRA, MRS WILLIE, VERNON, CHRISTEEN, JACK & MARGARET. BILL IS MAKING THE PHOTO. MADE ON ONE OF OUR TRIPS HOME IN THE 60TH. 2 FAMILY'S JOBS WERE FARMING, MILDRED'S HUSBAND WORK 2 SHIFT AT A FACTORY + FARMING & DEVELOPMENT, 2 FAMILY'S HAD MILITARY JOBS, 1 FAMILY HAD FACTORY JOBS, MR ADAMS JOB WAS WITH THE STATE HIGHWAY DEPARTMENT AND HE WALKED TO WORK.MRS ADAMS WAS A TEACHER AND FARMERS WIFE. MOST WERE VERY PRODUCTIVE AND BY HARD WORK AT THEIR JOBS CARVED OUT A VERY GOOD AND HAPPY LIFE. THEIR CHILDREN MOVING ON TO VERY GOOD JOB, As THE SAYING IS AN APPLE DOES NOT FALL FAR FROM THE TREE. AND ALSO TRAIN UP A CHILD IN THE WAY HE OR SHE SHOULD GO AND WHEN THEY ARE OLD THEY WILL NOT DEPART FROM IT. MOTHER, S JOB, S AS CEO OF THE HOME IS A JOB OFTEN OVERLOOKED. COOKING, SOWING, WASHING, CLEANING, PLUS HARD WORK, TRAINING THE CHILDREN RIGHT FROM WRONG IS PRICELESS. HAVE FAITH YOUR FAMILY WILL HAVE A WONDERFUL LIFE.

I LOVE THIS OPEN PLACE IN ATHENS GREECE WHERE THE APOSTLE PAUL SAW MANY STONE GODS AND HE USED THIS LOCATION TO TELL ABOUT HIS UNKNOWN GOD. THERE ARE MANY PLACES IN THIS USA WHERE WE CAN BUILD A PLACE LIKE THIS. HOWEVER TV, CELL PHONES, AND E-MAILS HAVE CHANGED THE WAY WE COMMUNICATE FOREVER. WE MAY WISH TO BUILD A PLACE LIKE THIS IN CASE A ELECTRICAL SOLAR STORM THAT WILL SHUT DOWN OUR MODES OF COMMUNICATION .IT WOULD TAKE A FEW JOBS TO DO IT. HAVE FAITH PEOPLE EVERY WHERE CAN SPEAK WITHOUT FEAR.

WE SPENT ONE CHRISTMAS IN THE GERMAN APARTMENTS BEFORE MOVING TO THE
GOVERNMENT APARTMENTS IN FRANKFORT GERMANY, ONE OF MY FIRST JOB, S WAS
FLYING TO BERLIN AND PERFORMING WORK AT THE AIRPORT. FROM OUR VANTAGE POINT
ON THE ROOF WE COULD LOOK OVER THE BERLIN WALL AND DOWN AT THE GUARDS IN
EAST GERMAN. THIS WAS THE WALL BUILT BY THE EAST GERMANS TO KEEP THEIR PEOPLE
IN. WOULD IT NOT BE GOOD IF WE COULD GET THE MEXICAN TO BUILD A WALL TO KEEP
PEOPLE IN AS WELL AS DRUGS. LET'S TALK ABOUT IT TO SAVE OUR MONEY. TIME CHANGES
THINGS. HAVE FAITH ALL PEOPLE IN THE WORLD ARE FREE.

JOB'S KEY TO BUYING HOME'S, HOME'S KEY TO JOBS

1.FOOD, CLOTHING, HOUSING 3 NECESSARY ITEMS IN LIFE . MY EARLY YEARS WERE JOBS AROUND GROWING FOOD. SOME OF MY JOB'S REQUIRED ME TO WEAR SPECIAL SAFETY SHOES, RUBBER AND LEATHER GLOVES FOR SAFETY AROUND HIGH VOLTAGE. SAFETY PROTECTION FOR MY EYES. MANY OF MY JOBS THROUGH THE YEARS HAVE BEEN AROUND HOUSING .INCLUDING ALL UTILITIES SUPPORTING HOUSING ELECTRICITY, WATER, GAS, PHONES, CABLE, PAINT, WOOD, CEMENT, BRICKS, STEEL, CARPET, PIPES, PAPER, FIXTURES, TANKS, HEATERS, AIR UNITS, ROOFING, AND ALL OTHER PARTS TO HOUSING. AT ONE TIME ONE OF MY JOB, S I WAS MAINTENANCE MANAGER OF 7296 HOUSING UNITS IN MEMPHIS AND HAD 12 MAINTENANCE SUPERVISOR WORKING FOR ME. ONE REASON I SELECTED TO BECOME A REAL ESTATE BROKER AND ONE EARLY SALE WAS 5 TRIPLEX UNITS, & 3 FOUR-PLEX UNITS. FOR 1.2 MILLION. MY NET COMMISSION WAS $ 48,000 AND I ARRANGED ALL FINANCING BETWEEN THE SELLERS & BUYERS ON THIS DEAL. HOUSING PROVIDE GOOD JOBS. HAVE FAITH THE WORLDS POPULATION FIND HOUSING THAT IS CONVERTED INTO HOMES.

THE 2ND FLOOR APARTMENT WAS OUR HOME FOR MOST OF THE TIME WHILE MY JOBS
KEEP ME MOVING FROM PLACE. JOB, S WORK WAS IN THIS ORDER.1ST A REHAB OR NEW JOB
WOULD BE DEVELOPED IN OUR ENGINEERING OFFICE. 2ND WE WOULD DRAW UP PLANS,
MAKE A MATERIAL LIST. 3RD ORDER THE PARTS & EQUIPMENT. 4TH FLY TO THE SITE TO
MAKE SURE THE SUPPLIES & EQUIPMENT WERE ON SITE. 5TH FLY THE CREW IN A DO THE
INSTALLATION JOB. REPEAT THE JOBS HAVE FAITH YOUR SKILLS WILL DO THE JOB AT HAND.

THIS CITY, BRAZIL WAS ABOUT 12 YRS OLD IN 1979 1.I HAD WANTED TO COME HERE AND IT WAS ALL I HAD WISHED FOR. ON A SATURDAY NIGHT AFTER LANDING I MEET LOCAL PEOPLE WHO ASK ME OUT TO CHURCH ON SUNDAY. AND ONCE WE ARRIVED AT CHURCH I WAS CALLED TO THE FRONT AND ASK TO SPEAK, AND I DID. THIS WAS ONE HIGHLIGHT OF MY VISIT HERE. WE ALSO HAD OUR OWN AIRCRAFT TO MOVE ABOUT THIS VAST COUNTRY. WE LANDED ON ONE RANCH THERE WAS A TENNESSEE MAN & HIS WIFE & ONE GERMAN MAN LIVING IN THE CENTER OF 60,000 AC. HE WAS RAISING CATTLE .THE HOUSE REALLY HAD NO WALLS AND THE KIDS HAD TO LIVE IN TOWN TO GO TO SCHOOL. MY EXTRA JOB THIS DAY WAS TO MAKE A ELECTRICAL REPAIR ON THE WATER PUMP ON THIS RANCH. I HAVE ALWAYS HAD A PLAN TO WORK WHERE EVER I LAND. I LOVED THIS VAST LAND .HAVE FAITH YOUR PLANS WORK OUT.

BEST JOB ON THIS EARTH IS TO SEE YOUR DAUGHTER MOVE TO THE TOP IN EDUCATION NOT ONLY IN BOOKS BUT TO THE TOP IN THE AREA OF LOOKS. OUR DAUGHTER MOTHER GETS THE CREDIT FOR THIS, JOB. THIS WAS OUR HUMBOLDT, TENNESSEE STRAWBERRY CELEBRATION. OUR DAUGHTER JOB IS WITH THE MTSU WHERE SHE HAS WORKED FOR THE PAST 18 YEARS AND HAS HELPED THOUSAND OF STUDENTS AS WELL AS THE JOB OF WATCHING ONE DAUGHTER, ONE SON, AND ONE DAUGHTERIN-LAW, GRADUATE FROM THIS UNIVERSITY .WOW WHAT A JOB. YOU GO VA FREEMAN ELLIS. HAVE FAITH YOUR CHILDREN WILL DO WELL.

AFTER HAVING MY FAMILY VISIT THIS LOCATION MY SONMADE A VISIT HERE AGAIN 40 YEARS LATER.

MY SON'S JOB ALLOWED HIM TO VISIT THIS SITE AS MY JOB HAD ALLOWED US TO VISIT THIS SAME PLACE 40 YEARS PRIOR. JOBS CHANGE, MAJOR SITES LIKE THE ARCH REMAIN THE SAME. PEOPLE AND CARS CHANGE GOVERNMENTS CHANGE, WHAT IS THE MEANING OF THIS. WARS COME AND GO, WE FIGHT FOR FREEDOM, MEN AND WOMEN WHO FIGHT AND MANY DIE, MANY LIVE, WHY? BECAUSE? WE TRY TO MAKE A GOOD OUTCOME THE USA IS CURRENTLY IN 3 WARS. I HAVE LIVED THROUGH WW II DEATH 291,557 WOUNDED 670,846 KOREAN CONFLICT DEATH 33,746,WONDED 103,284,VIETNAM CONFLICT DEAD,47,355 WOUNDED 153,284,OPERATION DESERT STORM DEATH 147 WOUNDED 467 OPERATION IRAQI FREEDOM DEATH 4481 WOUNDED 32,195 AFGHANISTAN 1748 DEATH 14342 WOUNDED, NOW NEW ACTION IN LIBYA NOW. OUTCOME GOOD? WAS IT, ALL WORTH IT YOU BET IT WAS & IS. FREEDOM HAS A PRICE, JACK'S JOBS AS YOUR JOBS ARE WORTH DOING. PUT YOUR HANDS TO WORK EVEN IF YOU HAVE TO BUILD BRICKS BY MOONLIGHT AND THANK GOD YOU HAVE A JOB.

1953 USAF 60 MILES INSIDE THE ARCTIC CIRCLE TWO MEN PER

ROOM 1 YEAR AWAY FROM YOUR WIFE & SON, NO CELL PHONE ONLY THE MAIL, NO TV MY JOB WAS RUNNING THE ELECTRICAL POWER PLANT, ALL RUNWAY LIGHTING, ALL EXTERIOR BASE & ALL INTERIOR BASE ELECTRICAL SYSTEMS SUPERVISOR OF 22 ELECTRICIAN 24 HRS PER DAY 7 DAYS PER WEEK, 365 DAYS IN 6O DEGREES BELOW ZERO 6 MO OF DARKNESS & 6 MO OF LIGHT. WHAT A JOB. THANKS TO A FINE USAF TECH SCHOOL AND MORE TRAINING AT 2 OTHER AIR BASE, S AND ONE RADAR SITE PRIOR TO ARRIVAL HERE I WAS READY FOR THE JOB. MY ROOM MATE, A PLUMBER WAS NOT MARRIED AND HIS PIN UP IS ABOVE HIS BED. EVERY MAN HAD A CALENDAR MARKING OFF EACH DAY UNTIL YOU WENT HOME. EVEN SO A YEAR WAS LIKE A LIFETIME. WORK WAS A GOOD FRIEND .KEEPING POWER ON FOR ABOUT 400 SOULS WITH OTHER VISITORS IN AND OUT CHANGING BEACON LIGHTS SOME OVER 1200 FT IN THE AIR WHAT A JOB GET ONE. HAVE FAITH YOUR HANDS CAN WORK ANY WHERE IN THIS WORLD .

FINDING A JOB IS LOOKING FOR A PROBLEM to FIX .1. WHEN I OBTAINED THIS JOB AS MANAGER. The system was uncompleted. THE 3 COMMISSIONERS, HAD FIRED THE PRIOR MANAGER. THEY OWED 12 MILLION IN BOND, S 2. There were 7 active lawsuits in progress. The 3 commissioners were about to go to jail, and the SEC had come in and removed all of our records. So I obtained an attorney drove to Atlanta Ga. Rented a copier to make copies 3. Now as Manger I knew what the SEC knew. They had placed an order where I could not buy or sell. I got around this order by Leasing New Trucks & Tractors, this permitted me to. 4. Extend the customer Base & also permitted more income. I found the US government, would not help until I reached a point where I did not need Help 5. After I did not need any help. Then I was able to obtain via FHA a government Loan. & The 3.6 M was used 1/2 to pay off the Bonds and 1/2 was used to contract out and completed the Project.6. Thus moving our Water District from a problem District to the best Water District in Tennessee. After This I resigned as Manager. So the Commissioners That I Had help to stay out of Jail. Lied and said I was Fired. This action caused me to lose 3 jobs until I found out & after producing my letter of resignation I then work 10 years a job. HAVE FAITH HARD TIMES WILL MAKE YOU A STRONGER PERSON.

ONE OF MY JOBS WAS TO MANAGE THE GIBSON CO WATER UTILITY. IT WAS IN A FAILED MODE WHEN I OBTAINED THE JOB. WE WERE ALMOST IN DEFAULT, UNFINISHED, AND WERE 12MILLION IN DEBT. ALSO WE HAD 7 LAWSUITS GOING AS WELL AS A SECURITY EXCHANGE COMMISSION INVESTIGATION IN PROGRESS,AND THEY HAD MOVED ALL OF OUR RECORD TO ATLANTA GA. I HIRED AN ATTORNEY WE TRAVELLED TO GA. AND UNDER THE FREEDOM OF INFORMATION ACT I RENTED A COPY MACHINE AND I MADE COPIES OF ALL OUR RECORDS AND IN SHORT I WAS ABLE TO OBTAIN A NEW FHA GOVERNMENT LOAN, PAY OFF THE TWO BONDS, AT 3.6 MILLION,WRITE OFF THE 12 MILLION, COMPLETE THE PROJECT, TAKING THE SYSTEM FROM THE WORST UTILITY TO THE BEST IN TENNESSEE. WE USED 1.6 M TO PAY OFF THE OLD BONDS & 1.6M TO COMPLETE IT. HAVE FAITH YOU CAN MAKE ALL YOU MANAGE LEFT IN A BETTER SHAPE BECAUSE OF YOUR EFFORT.

THE JOB AS MANAGER ALWAYS HAS MANY PROBLEMS. THE SECURITY & EXCHANGE
COMMISSION HAD GAVE THE ORDER WHERE I COULD NOT BUY OR SELL. TO KEEP
OPERATING I MADE A DEAL WITH A LOCAL FORD DEALER TO HELP ME LEASE A TRACTOR,&
NEW TRUCK THIS DEAL ALLOWED ME TO KEEP THE WATER SYSTEM WORKING UNTIL WE
COULD OBTAIN A $ 3.6 MILLION FHA LOAN . THE WATER SYSTEM, WAS SAVED FROM GOING
OUT OF BUSINESS, THE SYSTEM HAD 6 WATER TANKS, 12 WELLS, AND SUPPLIED WATER
TO ABOUT 10,000 PEOPLE. AFTER OBTAINING THE LOAN WE USED A CONTRACTOR TO
COMPLETE THE SYSTEM, AT THE TIME MY WORKER WERE TWO OFFICE PERSONNEL, ONE
FORMAN, ONE METER READER,AND 3 OTHER WORKER. ALL WERE EXCELLENT WORKERS. ALL
JOBS WERE SAVED, AFTER MANY YEARS SOME PERSONAL STILL THERE. HAVE FAITH EVERY
JOB YOU HAVE WILL BRING A BETTER LIFE TO ALL YOU SERVE.

JOSH'S WIFE PAULA, WENDY & CAMI CHRISTMAS TIME. ONEGOOD THING, WATCH YOUR
CHILDREN GROW. PAULA JOB IS A TEACHER. WENDI JOB IS A HUMAN RESOURCE MANAGER.
CAMI JOB IS A DENTAL ASSISTANCE .ALL JOB, S REQUIRE TIME OFF FOR THE HOLIDAYS AND
VISIT, S HOME FOR FAMILY FOOD & FUN. OUR WHOLE FAMILY HAS BEEN TRULY BLESSED
WITH GOOD HEALTH, GOOD LOOK, S, GOOD BRAINS, GOOD EDUCATION, AND MOST OF ALL
GOOD HOMES. THE TOTAL LIFE IS MARRIAGE BRINGS CHILDREN THEN GRAND CHILDREN,
THEN GREAT GRAND CHILDREN, WHAT MORE CAN YOU WANT IN LIFE? HAVE FAITH YOUR
FAMILY ALWAYS FIND PEACE & HAPPINESS.

My Hands at work in Greenland

While in the USAF in Greenland My Job was to keep all Lights Burning. We had two Radio Towers over 1200 feet high. I climbed the tower without any Safety gear and replaced the light Bulbs on the tower, I was a young Air Force Staff Sgt. In charge of About 22 Air Force Electrical airman. Because I was in charge it was my job because no one else would Do it. We also ran the Power House to supply all base Power I have always gone where others fear to Go. Of course the Contractors who built the Towers also had no fear, Electrical Power & Communication Have been a much of my hands work.

AT THE EDGE OF THE GREENLAND ICE CAP IN 1953. WE WALKED FROM SONDERSTOM
AIR BASE AT THIS TIME IT WAS ALSO MELTING AND A RIVER WAS RUNNING AROUND THE
EDGE WITH LARGE CHUNKS BREAKING OF AND FALLING IN THE RIVER I BELIEVE WE WERE
LOCATED 60 MILES INSIDE THE ARTIC CIRCLE. AND AS I RECALL WE WALKED ABOUT 15 MILES
FROM THE BASE TO GET TO THE EDGE AND MAKE A FEW PICTURES .IT WAS CRAZY FOR US
TO BE HERE WITH NO PROTECTION FROM THE POLO BEARS IN THE AREA. HOWEVER BEING
YOUNG MANY TIMES YOU ACT WITH OUT MUCH THINKING ABOUT DANGERS. WHAT A JOB.
I LATER DEVELOPED A STANDARD IN MY LIFE TO LINK THOUGHTS WITH ACTIONS. SOME
PEOPLE THINK AND NEVER ACT. SOME PEOPLE ACT AND NEVER THINK .GET A JOB. HAVE.
HAVE FAITH THE ICE WILL NOT ALL MELT

MY SON AND ONE OF HIS TOYS HE LOVES TO RIDE. HIS JOB IS TO HELP BUILD AND BRING ON LINE FACTORIES IN THE USA & AROUND THE WORLD. HE BOUGHT THIS TOY AFTER MAKING SEVERAL TRIPS TO CHINA AND BY NOW HAS PLACED ABOUT 40 THOUSAND MILES ON IT. FLYING, DRIVING, RIDING THIS IRON HORSE IS A MAJOR UPGRADE FROM THE REAL HORSE I RODE TO SCHOOL IN THE 40, S AND THE SCOOTER I RODE TO NIGHT SCHOOL IN CALIFORNIA IN THE 50TH.LIFE BRINGS GOOD JOBS TO ALL WHO DEVELOP A SKILL LEVEL THAT IS WORTH PURE GOLD TO ANY COMPANY WHO UNDERSTAND THE TRUE VALUE OF A PERSON WHO CAN USE THEIR MIND AND HANDS .GET ANY ASSIGNED JOB DONE. IF YOU REALLY WANT A JOB DEVELOP A NEEDED SKILL .HAVE FAITH YOUR HANDS & KNOWLEDGE WILL LAST YOUR LIFETIME.

SUNRISE & SUNSET LAND & WATER UP AND DOWN

JOBS ARE NEEDED 24 HRS ROUND THE CLOCK, WHILE THE LUCKY OLD SUN KEEPS MOVING
AROUND WITHOUT OUR HELP. GOD MADE HEAVEN & EARTH GIVING US WATER AND LAND.
AS I WAS FLYING AROUND THE WORLD,AND MY JOBS ALLOWING ME TO SPEND TIME
CLOSE TO THE NORTH POLE, AND IN THE HOT JUNGLE MEETING PEOPLE IN MOST OF THE
LARGE CITIES I HAVE FOUND PEOPLE WITH MANY GODS IWONDER WHY WE BELIEVE WHAT
WE BELIEVE ? I HAVE MET PEOPLE WHO DO NOT BELIEVE IN ANY GOD. WHAT IS THE TRUE
MEANING OF ALL THIS? I HAVE ALWAYS FOUND BY LOOKING UP, LISTING UP, SHUTTING UP,
STANDING UP, SPEAKING UP, ABOUT ALL THE WONDERFUL PLACES AROUND, GIVE ME FAITH
IN MY GOD. I BELIEVE A PERSON WHO HAS NO GOD IS DRESSED UP WITH NO PLACE TO GO.

ALL WOMEN I KNOW HAVE MUCH BEAUTY I ALSO KNOW IFTHEY ARE STONE COLD, LEAVE!

WE LIVE NEXT DOOR TO A FINE ARTIST WHO SOLD HIS ART AT UP TO $10,000 A PAINTING, THIS WAS HIS ONLY JOB, WELL HE ALSO DID SOME SONG WRITING. HE SAID A WOMAN ASK HIM COULD HE PAINT HER IN THE NUDE, HE SAID I GUESS SO IF YOU WILL LET ME KEEP MY SOCKS ON, SO I CAN CLEAN MY PAINT BRUSH, S. WE FOUND MUCH ART IN MANY PLACES IN THIS WORLD. AND I TAKE MY HAT OFF TO ALL THE ART IN THIS WORLD.NOW WE HAVE MADE PROGRESS TO THE POINT A CELL PHONE WILL MAKE A FINE PHOTO AND SEND IT IN A FLASH AROUND THE WORLD, WHAT A JOB .CAN A FARM BOY FROM TENNESSEE ENJOY ART. YES JUST FIND YOU A JOB THAT WILL LET YOU TRAVEL THE WORLD AND YOU WILL FIND ART IN MANY LOCATIONS. COMMUNICATION IS A WONDERFUL JOB.IN MANY JOBS YOU WILL FIND TRAVEL AND LOOK FOR ART ON YOUR DAYS OFF. HAVE FAITH ARTIST HANDS WILL BUILD FINE ART.

11.21.2010 17:0

GRANDSON JOSH, GRANDDAUGHTER WENDI, HAPPY.1

JOB IS TO SEE YOUR FAMILY GROW. WENDI STARTED HER JOB WORKING AT KROGER WHEN SHE WAS GOING TO MTSU, SHE OBTAIN HER DEGREE IN HUMAN RESOURCE AND WORK MANY JOBS, SHE WAS A COMPUTER HEAD HUNTER, MOVING AROUND AND AT ONE TIME WORKED WITH A PLACE IN AIG. MOVING TO HER CURRENT JOB AND AS A SINGLE MOM WITH ONE DAUGHTER HAS BOUGHT HER THIRD HOME A VERY GOOD ONE IN NASHVILLE TENNESSEE. TOUGH AS STEEL, BRIGHT AS THE SUN, AND SMART AS THE THEY COME, WITH A HEART OF GOLD. JOSH OUR MIDDLE GRANDSON COMPLETED MTSU AND MARRIED LAST YEAR. FOR WHATEVER REASON JOSH HAS CHOSE A JOB OF LAYING HARDWOOD FLOORS, AND HIS WIFE PAULA IS A TEACHER. MY THINKING IS EVERY PERSON FINDS (WHATSOEVER JOB YOU FIND AND ARE HAPPY DOING IT DO IT WITH ALL YOUR MIGHT) STEVE JOSH, S DAD HAS WORKED FOR YEARS AS A LINEMAN WITH BELLSOUTH. HE HAS BEEN A FINE SON IN LAW AND WONDERFUL FATHER. WHAT MORE IN LIFE CAN YOU ASK FOR. A GOOD BALL GAME, A GOOD STEAK, A GOOD NAP. LOVE YOUR KIDS AND GRANDKIDS. MAKE IT TO RETIREMENT VACATION OFTEN. HAVE FAITH YOUR FAMILY WILL FIND GOOD JOB, S

ONE SPECIAL HOME IN OVER LOOKING THE CITY & HARBOR IN KOBE JAPAN.

THIS WAS OFF BASE TEMPORARY HOUSING WHEN MY FAMILY JOINED ME IN JAPAN. IT WAS LOCATED ABOUT HALF WAY UP A MOUNTAIN AND YOU HAD A WONDERFUL VIEW OF THE CITY WHERE YOU COULD LOOK AT THE SHIPS COMING INTO KOBE HARBOR . THE HOME WAS OWNER WAS A WOMAN WITH A PRIOR MARRIAGE TO AN AMERICAN, HOWEVER SHE MOVED BACK IN WITH HER FAMILY AND RENTED HER HOME TO US. THERE WAS A CABLE CAR UP THE HILL THAT YOU COULD RIDE UP THE MOUNTAIN. IT WAS A SMALL HOME THAT WAS EQUIPPED WITH A SPECIAL GAS HEATER THAT HEATED THE WATER ONLY AS YOU USED IT. YOU SAVED MONEY BECAUSE IT WAS ONLY USED GAS AS YOU NEED HOT WATER. I REMEMBER THE YOUNG LOCAL CHILDREN WORE SCHOOL UNIFORMS. IT WAS SMALL HOWEVER IT WAS SPECIAL LOCATION FOR MY WIFE MARGARET, SON MARK, DAUGHTER VIRGINIA WHILE I WORKED AT ONE OF JACK, S JOBS AT THE ITAMI AIR BASE THAT LATER BECAME OSAKA AIR PORT. HAVE FAITH TO MAKE ANY HOUSE YOUR HOME.

WORLD'S TALLEST BUILDING DUBAI

THE CITY OF DUBIA HAS BEEN A GENERATOR OF MANY JOBS. IN REALITY IT ONE OF THE NEW WORLD CITIES.THESE APARTMENT UNITS ALSO HAVE THE PRAYER TOWERS ATTACHED HANDY FOR LIVING AND WORSHIPING. THIS IS ALSO THE CITY & HOME OF THE WORLD, S HIGHEST BUILDING. IT WAS BUILT IN 4 YEARS, MANY JOBS HERE NOT ONLY FOR US WORKERS BUT FOR WORKERS FROM ALL OVER THE WORLD.

THE JOB MAKING PLACE HAS TO BE THIS PLACE & THE EARLY DAYS WE WERE ON OUR WAY TO A NEW JOB AT TACOMA WASHINGTON IN OUR 1957 CHEV. LIFE IS ALWAYS A GAMBLE

JOBS   COMING UP FOR ME WAS A VERY GOOD SCHOOL, THE TRAINING WAS ACCOMPLISHED BY EX NAVY MEN WORKING FOR A CONTRACTOR EMPLOYED BY THE US AIR FORCE BECAUSE THE SYSTEM WE WERE GOING TO OPERATE WAS A COMPLEX STAND ALONE ELECTRICAL, AIR, LARGE GENERATORS AND PROVIDING STABLE POWER TO COMPLEX ELECTRONIC SYSTEMS WATCHING ANY INCOMING ICBM OR AIRCRAFT. OUR SYSTEMS WOULD OPERATE IF THERE WAS NO OUTSIDE ELECTRICAL POWER OR GAS LINES. IT WAS A VERY GOOD DESIGN FOR THE TIMES .THESE WERE THE DAYS OF HUGE COMPUTER SYSTEMS, REQUIRING MASSIVE AIR CONDITIONS SYSTEMS, AND MOTOR GENERATION FOR STABLE POWER. THIS WAS YESTERDAY, TODAY MOST EVERYTHING HAS CHANGED. HAVE FAITH YOUR CARS WILL TAKE YOU ANY WHERE.

MY WIFE AND DAUGHTER TWO BLONDS IN A WORLD MOSTLY BLACK HAIRED JAPANESE
PEOPLE LOOKING.

THE FREEMAN FAMILY AT MY 80TH BIRTHDAY PARTY. A FAMILY OF MANY AFTER A 60 YEAR
MARRIAGE WHAT A GREAT GROUP OF WORKING HANDS DOING MANY JOB,S WITH SKILLS
DEVELOP BY EDUCATION, SELF TRAINING AND APPLICATION OF USING THE MIND AND
WORK TO MAKE HOMES OUT OF HOUSING BRINGING ALONG LITTLE ONES TO REPLACE THE
TWO JACK & MARGRET WHO MARRIED IN 1952.WE HAD OUR SON & DAUGHTER EARLY ON
AND THEY WERE EDUCATED OVER THE WORLD AS WE SPENT 12 YEARS OVERSEAS.& IT NO
WONDER MY SON PROGRESS TO PROJECT MANAGER FOR A MAJOR COMPANY BUILDING
FOOD PLANTS AROUND THE WORLD HELPING TO PROVIDE FOOD FOR MILLIONS USING
HIS MIND AND HANDS IN HIS JOBS SKILLS,DEVELOPED BY HARD WORK AND BEING MAINLY
SELF TRAINED .WHILE OUR DAUGHTER HAS WORKED IN A MAJOR TENNESSEE UNIVERSITY
HELPING STUDENTS OBTAIN A DEGREE BY THE THOUSANDS IN THE PAST 18 YEARS, MANY
JOBS BY MANY HANDS IN THIS PHOTO. HAVE FAITH ALL OF YOUR FAMILIES WILL FINDS JOBS
AS OUR FAMILY HAS FOUND JOBS GOD BLESS THE USA .AND ALL OF THE PEOPLE IN OUR
WORLD.

GIBSON CO. COURT HOUSE TRENTON TENNESSEE

1. EVERY CENTER OF GOVERMENT HAS A COURT HOUSE, AND IS A NUMBER 1 JOB GENERATOR OF GOOD JOBS, NOW AS YOU DRIVE AROUND TRENTON YOU SEE A TOWN WITH MOST SMALL STORES GONE, SOME DOWN TOWN BANK GONE, GOVERMENT JOBS. STILL GREAT. WALMARK AND TARGET HAS REPLACED THE STORES THAT ONCE WAS HERE, WITH THE CHAMBER OF COMMERCE STILL WORKIN TO BRING IN NEW JOBS. WHERE 2 POLICEMAN USE TO DO THE JOB & BABE HARDWOOD & ONE # 2 LEAD PENCILE DID MOST OF THE RECORD & A YELLOW LINE TABLET, FOR THE CITY, FOR THE MOST PART. OUR TOWN HAS CHANGED FROM THE PAST.ITS STILL MY HOME TOWN & I JUST BOUGHT A PRIOR DENTAL OFFICE NEXT TO THE POST OFFICE. LOOK AT THE NEW CITY HALL & THE RE-WORKED COURT HOUSE & THE WORLD, S LARGEST GROUP OF NIGHT LIGHTED TEA POTS.BEING THE CENTER OF GIBSON CO IS A GREAT PLACE FOR THE COURT HOUSE AND MANY FINE GOVERNMENT JOB, S. LOTS OF HISTORY HERE.TIMES HAS CHANGED HOWEVER I REMBER THE SODA FOUNTANS,10C MOVIES A GREAT PLACE YESTERDAY & TODAY AS WELL.

FAMILY BONDING JOB RIDING 4 WHEELERS 1.FOR SEVERAL YEAR NOW MY SON &
GRANDSON, HAVE MADE TIME TO GO TO THE MOUNTIANS AND RIDE FOR TWO OR THREE
DAYS. MANY TIMES THEY ARE JOINED WITH OTHER FRIENDS. I KNOW OF NO BETTER JOB
THAN TO TAKE A BREAK FROM YOUR REAL JOB AND SPEND TIME IN THE WILD WITH THE
BLACK BEARS AND MOUNTIAN RATTLERS. THERE IS MORE TO LIFE THAN THE DAILEY GRIND
AT YOUR REAL JOB. MANY COUNTRIES OUTSIDE THE USA HAVE MANY MORE DAYS AWAY
FROM THEIR JOBS THAN WE DO IN THE USA. FROM THE COOLERS I, AM SURE THEY WERE
NOT THIRSTY.

EIGHTY YEARS OF HOMES LIST & A GOOD LIFE.

1ST FARM HOME & BARN. 2ND HOME (STORE ACROSS THE ROAD) 3RD & 4th WERE

TWO RENTAL HOMES IN SAN ANGELO TEXAS.5TH HOME WAS IN ROCKVILLE INDIANA.6TH

MY WIFE MOVED BACK WITH MY MOM & DAD WHILE I SPENT A YEAR IN GREENLAND.7TH &

8TH HOMES WERE IN SPOKAN WASHINGTON. MOVED BACK TO 10TH   A RENTAL HOME

IN TN. 11TH HOME A DUPLEX AT STEWART AFB TN.NEXT HOME 12TH A RENTAL IN KOBA

JAPAN. 13TH IN HAMADERA JAPAN .14TH HOME WAS IN YOKATO JAPAN . 15TH WAS A

RENTAL IN FLORIDA . WE BOUGHT OUR 16TH HOME IN TOCAMA WASHINGTON . 17TH WAS

GOVERNMENT HOUSING AT McCORD AFB. 18th a RENTAL IN SAN BERDIANO CALIF. 19TH

HOME WAS A RENTAL IN FRANKFORT GERMANY . 20TH & 21TH (SAME BUILDING) GOV,

HOUSING IN FRANKFORT GERMANY.22TH WE BOUGH OUR 2ND HOME IN FORT WALTON

FLA.23RD HOME WAS GOVERNMENT HOUSING AT KESLER AFB IN MISS.24TH HOME WAS A

RENTAL ON OKINAWA . 25TH HOME WAS A GOVERNMENT HOUSE AT NAHA AFB OKINAWA,

26TH HOME WAS A GOVERNMENT HOUSE AT TOPEKA KANSAS . BOUGHT OUR 27TH HOUSE

IN TRENTON TN. BOUGHT OUR 28TH HOME IN MEMPHIS TN. BOUGHT OUR 29TH HOME

IN TRENTON TN. BOUGHT OUR 30TH HOME IN TRENTON TN. MOVED BACK TO OUR 29TH

HOME. BOUGHT OUR 31TH HOME IN SPRINGFIELD TN. (MY BEST HOME). BOUGHT OUR 32TH

IN TRENTON TN. BOUGHT OUR 33rd IN JACKSON TN. AND WE STILL IN IT. WE HAVE LIVED IN

MANY MOTELS, AND SOME RENTAL HOMES ARE NOT LISTED. ITS BEEN OVERALL A GREAT

LIFE. HAVE FAITH ALL OF YOUR HOUSES WILL BE CONVERTED BY YOUR WIFE (62 YRS OF

MARRIAGE INTO A HOME.

JACK,

I was trying to think of something unique to give you on your eightieth birthday. You are a special person to me and I wanted your gift to be special too.

I decided to give you a trip. Don't go search for your passport or start packing a bag. You can take this little journey from the comfort of your recliner. I hope you enjoy this gift from me to you.

I am proud to be your son-in-law, and I am fortunate to have known you for these past thirty-six years. Love, Steve Ellis   10-2011

Born during the "Great Depression". President Hoover was in a twit trying to put America back to work. Times were hard for most of the population. You were lucky to be born into a farming family. At least you knew where your next meal was coming from. We all know how much you hate to miss a meal. And with all the sisters you had, you must have been spoiled rotten in your early years. In 1931, the Empire State Building was completed in New York City. The gangster Al Capone was put in jail for tax evasion.

In 1936 you were five years old. You may not remember a lot from that year. Hoover Dam was completed on the border between Arizona and Nevada. At the time, it was the largest concrete structure ever built. The novel "Gone with the Wind" was published for the first time. The Spanish Civil War began. And the Olympics opened in Berlin Germany. These were the first ever to be televised live.

In 1938 you were seven. Oil was discovered in Saudi Arabia. I wish you could have gotten in on that. Europe was in turmoil. War is coming soon with Germany. Also that year the racehorse Seabiscuit won his famous race at Pimlico race track beating War Admiral by four lengths.

In 1940 you were nine. The war in Europe was getting worse every day. Winston Churchill gave his famous "We shall never surrender" speech. Paris falls to Germany and the Battle of Britain begins. Food rationing begins in England.

In 1941 you turned ten years old. I'm sure you probably remember some of the things that were happening then. The war in Europe was still being fought. The German battleship Bismarck was sunk, killing 2,300 people. But for certain, the Japanese attack on Pearl Harbor was the biggest thing to happen to the U.S in 1941. Do you remember that?

In 1944 you were thirteen. I guess the biggest thing that happened that year was the Battle of Normandy, or D-Day as it was called then. 155,000 Allied forces landed in France and in short order liberated Paris. It also weakened the German position in Europe. The Allied forces seize control of Florence, Italy. They also liberate Brussels. And that year, Roosevelt became the first and last president to be elected for a fourth term.

In 1944 you turned fourteen. The Jewish concentration camp begins to be liberated in Europe. President Roosevelt dies and Truman becomes the thirty-third president. Hitler commits suicide in a bunker.

In 1946 you turned fifteen years old. For the most part, the war in Europe was over. The United Nations held its first meeting in London. The Bank of England is nationalized. The Nuremberg trials were ongoing. Nazi war criminals are hung for their crimes. And a small company, Tokyo Telecommunications Engineering, was founded with only twenty employees. Later the name was changed to The Sony Corporation. And Harry Truman officially ended the hostilities of WWII.

In 1947 you were sixteen. That year Princess Elizabeth (now Queen Elizabeth) gets engaged to Prince Philip and later in the year, they married. India gains its independence from England. President Truman signs the national Security Act which creates the CIA, the Department of Defense, the Joint Chiefs of Staff and the National Security Council.

In 1949 you turned eighteen. That year Joe Louis, the heavyweight champion, retired from boxing. The Peoples Republic of China was established.

In 1950 you were nineteen. The Korean (conflict) War began when North Korean troops crossed the 38th parallel into South Korea. In November, China joined in the fighting with North Korea against us.

In 1951 you turned twenty. That year, the United Nations relocated to New York City. The comic strip "Dennis the Menace" began appearing in newspapers across America. President Truman officially declares and end to the war with Germany. The novel "Catcher in the Rye" by J.D. Salinger is published. But the best news of the year had to be the birth, on March 18th, of Steve Ellis.

And finally in 1952, you turned to the legal age of twenty-one. I'm pretty sure you remember that milestone. Elizabeth II is proclaimed Queen of England. The Winter Olympics was held in Oslo, Norway. The summer Olympics were held in Helsinki, Finland.

Well Jack, I hope that you have enjoyed this little trip back to your past. You have certainly been around for some of the most exciting things. All the wonderful inventions of the past eighty years are mind boggling. All the accomplishments our country has made from putting a man on the moon to unimaginable leaps in technology, you've seen it all. I'm sure there's a lot more to come. Happy 80th Birthday!!!

DO YOU REMEMBER THIS ?????

1932= Amelia Earhart flies across the U.S and the Atlantic Ocean. Ronald Reagan graduates from college.

1933= Prohibition Law repealed. Bonnie and Clyde are starting their reign of lawlessness. But not for long.

1934= Hitler comes to power in Germany. Outlaws John Dillinger and Bonnie and Clyde are eliminated.

1935=Elvis Presley born. Sinatra gets his start in the business. Babe Ruth plays last major league game.

1937= The Golden Gate Bridge openedfor traffic.The Hindenburg explodes. A. Earhart is missing in flight.

 1942= U.S. begins A-Bomb research. Cassius Clay and Aretha Franklin born. Daylight Savings Time begins

1943= The Pentagon is completed. The WPA   ends. Eisenhower named Supreme Allied Commander.

1948= Israel declared an independent state. NASCAR has first stock car at Daytona Beach.

1953= Polio vaccine successfully used.

1954= First issue of Sports illustrated.

1955= Disneyland opens in California.

1956= Elvis's first hit Heartbreak Hotel.

1957= American Bandstand debuts on ABC.

1958= Wham-0 invents the Hula-Hoop.

1959= Alaska and Hawaii become states.

1960= John F. Kennedy wins presidential election

1961= Disposable diapers Pampers invented.

1962= First Walmart opened in Arkansas.

1963= Kennedy shol Alcatraz closes.

1964= Ford makes the first Mustang.

1965= Medicare starts in U.S. Mini skirt appears.

1966= Star Trek first broadcast on television

1967= First Super Bowl-Packers beat Chiefs35-10

1968= Robert Kennedy-Martin L. King shot dead.

1969= Apollo lands first man on the moon.

1970= The Beatles break up. The EPA begins.

1971= Voting age lowered to 18 in U.S.

1972= Atari releases first video game PONG

1973= United States withdraws from Vietnam.

1974= Pocket calculators go on sale to the public.

1975= Jack and Margaret's daughter is wed.

1976= Apple Computer company formed.

1977= US turns Panama Canal over to Panama.

1978= Volkswagen Beetle stops production.

1979= First Bungee Jumping happens in England

1980= Mt. St. Helens erupts in Washington state.

1981= Post-It notes introduced. Reagan elected.

1982= Disney's Epcot Center opens in Florida.

1983= Final episode of TV show "Mash"

1984= Communications giant AT&T broken up.

1985= Microsoft releases Windows 1.0

1986= Space Shuttle "Challenger" lost on launch.

1987= Disposable contact lenses introduced.

1988= Stealth Bomber, Hubble Telescope, Prozac

1989= Berlin Wall falls. Cold War ends.

1990= Iraq invades Kuwait. U.S. goes to war.

1991= Airbags introduced in US automobiles.

1992= Clinton elected. NAFTA enacted.

1993= Beanie Babies. World Wide Web begins.

1994= Lisa Ma.rie Presley weds Michael Jackson.

1995= Oklahoma City Federal Building bombed.

1996= E-bay website introduced on internet.

1997= Princess Diana dies. China gets Hong Kong

1998= The search engine "Google" is founded.

1999= Euro becomes single currency in Europe.

2000= Bush defeats Gore by a hair for president.

2001= 9-11-World Trade Center destroyed

2002= Department of Homeland Security formed.

2003= U.S. invades Iraq. Shuttle "Columbia" lost

2004= Tsunami across coastal Asia kills 200k

2005= Hurricane "Katrina" destroys Gulf coast

2006= Planet Pluto declared not to be a planet

2007= Apple unveils the iPhone

2008= Sub prime mortgage crisis begins

2009= Obama elected. Michael Jackson dies

2010= Chilean miners rescued after 68 days

2011= Jack Freeman turns the BIG Eight- Ooh

2012= The Diamond Jubilee of Queen Elizabeth2013=North Korea conducts its third nuclear test

2014=Google Glass is launched to the public

HAPPY BIRTHDAY JACK FREEMAN

I hope you enjoyed reading the last four pages, and that you have a wonderful day.

Printed in the United States
By Bookmasters